purposeful
curiosity

purposeful curiosity

The Power of Asking the Right Questions at the Right Time

DR. CONSTANTINE ANDRIOPOULOS

hachette
BOOKS

NEW YORK

Hachette Go, an imprint of Hachette Books
Hachette Book Group
1290 Avenue of the Americas
New York, NY 10104
HachetteGo.com
Facebook.com/HachetteGo
Instagram.com/HachetteGo

First Edition: October 2022
Hachette Books is a division of Hachette Book Group, Inc.

The Hachette Go and Hachette Books name and logos are trademarks of Hachette Book Group, Inc.

The publisher is not responsible for websites (or their content) that are not owned by the publisher.

Print book interior design by Linda Mark.

Library of Congress Control Number: 2022942380

ISBN: 9780306847363 (hardcover), 9780306847387 (ebook)

Printed in the United States of America

LSC-C

Printing 1, 2022

To Lydia,
the most curious girl in the world

Contents

Preface

> *The mind is not a vessel to be filled, but a fire*
> *to be kindled.*
>
> —PLUTARCH

IT WAS A WARM SUMMER AFTERNOON ON MYKONOS, A GREEK ISLAND known for its picturesque town, gorgeous beaches, and vibrant nightlife. Iraklis Zisimopoulos, my best friend, whom I have known since we were both seven years old, and I were talking about his new hospitality ventures on the island. At one point, he interrupted our conversation, turned to me, and said, "You must be the most annoying person in the world!" I was taken aback by his comment. Puzzled, I asked, "What do you mean?"

"You fire one hundred questions per minute. I can't stand you!" he replied laughing. "We're supposed to be having a quiet afternoon, and you act like an investigator. What will you do with all this information, anyway? Will you ever use it?"

"I don't know," I replied. "I find what you're doing quite interesting, but to be honest, it's doubtful that I'll use any of what you're telling me."

Guilty as charged: I am a curious person, actively engaged in the act of learning and exploring.[1] Perhaps I'm a bit too curious at times. Academics are like children. We share an unwieldy curiosity, but I had never thought of it as a problem, and so the conversation with my friend hit a chord. It bothered me for a while, but when the summer ended and I returned to London in the fall to teach at Bayes Business School, that summer day with my friend became a distant memory.

Throughout my professional life, I have been deeply invested in helping people advance their curiosity into new and better ways to live and create. This goal has served me well in my present roles at Bayes Business School (City, University of London): as professor of innovation and entrepreneurship, associate dean for entrepreneurship, and investment committee member of Bayes Entrepreneurship Fund (the school's venture capital fund). My passion for curiosity also informs my work as director of Avyssos Advisors Ltd., an innovation management consultancy, and as a business consultant and coach.

My mission is to inspire a movement that awakens purposeful curiosity as the foundation of innovation. I am personally invested in this cause because I am a father and an educator.

During the semester, I noticed that many of my students drifted from topic to topic, wanting to discover more about what they were learning but without the patience to drill down deeply into a specific subject. Their interest seemed superficial at best. My recognition of this tendency reminded me of the summer conversation I had with my old friend. I realized that my students didn't know how to channel their curiosity in a way that was useful for discovery and ideation. They didn't keep asking questions about a specific topic; they just moved on to the next thing.

Like many of us, they are distracted by the flood of information we are bombarded with through social media, newsletters, texts, email, and streaming services. They become like butterflies, flitting from flower to flower without landing on one long enough to drink deeply of its nectar.

We are the generation of right now. Instant gratification is expected because of the ease with which we can distract ourselves and the ton of information at our fingertips. We can order both food and romance from the comfort of our sofas. Technology has made us more complacent and draws us to an ever-increasing comfort zone. Streaming entertainment services, food delivery, and dating apps support the ecosystem of convenience.

> *When we dedicate considerable time to investigate, to find answers beyond the first glance, the obvious or expected can be exhilarating and deeply satisfying.*

The facts back me up: The internet has given us unprecedented access to knowledge that grows, like our curiosity, exponentially each year. There are 2.5 quintillion (a quintillion is a million trillion) bytes of data created each day.[2] Google search queries increase around 10 percent per year.[3] Out of trillions of searches every year, 15 percent of our queries are original, having never been seen by Google before.[4] Around 3.5 billion people carry a smartphone.[5] The average American checks their phone 344 times a day.[6] Most people, on average, spend 3 hours and 19 minutes a day on their phones.[7] In 2020, we spent, on average, 7 hours per day online.[8] In 2020, daily social media usage was 145 minutes per day.[9]

I can be guilty of indulging in social media distraction, too. Like my students, I use my personal technology to go on aimless internet searches about both important and unimportant topics, gaining superficial knowledge before moving on to the next thing. The upside is convenience and novelty. The downside is that we can lose interest in any journey that takes more than a few minutes and a few clicks on our smartphones.

The easy access to ever-growing portals of information has created ideal conditions to satisfy our innate curiosity while at the same time encouraging a superficiality that prevents us from doing deep dives into subjects. Despite the rapid pace of technological advancements and the ease with which we can now find information instantly on our own for many topics, we are not witnessing an equivalent surge in deep curiosity journeys. In fact, the easy access to information and our connectedness seems to have had the opposite result. We have become addicted to breadth over depth, worshipping quick and straightforward answers. We want to know the answers to things even when there is no apparent benefit. In this book, I call this attitude *frivolous curiosity*. A recent study by Ming Hsu, a neuro-economist from University of California, Berkeley's Haas School of Business, and his team reported that our brains can overestimate the value of information that makes us feel good but that may not be useful.[10] Don't get me wrong. In the right amounts, frivolous curiosity can be highly beneficial. It can help us leave the known path and experiment. Learning by chance something today may be helpful tomorrow. It's not that I am against this approach, but it should not be the norm. Why is going deep with our interest in a given subject or problem becoming more challenging than it was in the past? What is preventing us from channeling our curiosity more deeply and toward a defined purpose?

I decided to discover why this butterfly approach to intellectual exploration was growing and what it might mean for innovation, business, and the future. More importantly, I wanted to learn how we could become more intentional about the benefits of going deeper. This book is the result of that undertaking. It lifts the veil on the way accomplished individuals channel their curiosity to a particular purpose—toward advancing science and human understanding, discovering new lands and opportunities, or reaching a significant goal. This is what I call *purposeful curiosity*, the kind that gets you off your couch and propels you to solve complex puzzles. It is about immersing yourself into the unknown with clarity, passion, courage, and a positive, enterprising attitude. This kind of curiosity requires effort, patience, and resources and may lead you to exhaustion, but it is also overwhelmingly meaningful, rewarding, transformative, and, often, fun. Purposeful curiosity has tremendous benefits. Curiosity—the urge to know, to see, or to experience—is what motivates information-seeking behavior.[11] This drive has long been associated with positive emotions, lower levels of anxiety, strengthened relationships, achievement, and longevity.[12]

Purposeful curiosity helps steer inquisitiveness toward goals that we care about and that give meaning to everything we do. By solving puzzles along our journey, we often uncover diverse new pathways, surfacing ideas, problems, and solutions that may be loosely related to the mystery and each other. The path to the destination, and even the destination itself, may be unclear. I won't claim that purposeful curiosity is always fun; it can be, of course, and it can also be difficult and frustrating. But that is where its value is. When we dedicate considerable time to investigate, to find answers beyond the first glance, the obvious or expected can be exhilarating and deeply satisfying. For a space explorer, successfully launching a rocket is an immense and complex challenge. For an Olympic athlete, winning a gold medal means a lifetime of hard work, both physical and mental, but the effort is worth it. For a soprano, hitting the right note is exceptionally difficult. For most of us, devoting sustained attention toward a challenging purpose is an arduous task! Yet, moving beyond your original boundaries of knowledge and skill is its own deeply satisfying reward.

In this fuzzy process, a concentrated effort to overcome obstacles, to eliminate mental resistance with resilience, plays a key role. Masters of purposeful curiosity develop an ability to sustain focus and attention. I have talked with several of these experts for this book. The resulting insights will help put you in their shoes and let you feel their triumphs and tribulations. You will discover the hidden threats to their journeys, the setbacks (even the disasters) they've experienced, and how they mitigate all these challenges to successfully reach their destination. Many of us romanticize the idea of embarking on the unknown. Actually, purposeful curiosity is more like waking up every morning, walking into a boxing arena with Mike Tyson, not knowing if you will take him down or if you'll get punched in the face. Sometimes the work goes smoothly, but more often you will meet frustration that takes grit and determination to survive.

The purposefully curious have learned to overcome setbacks—and learn from them—and leverage them for success. Working through problems without distraction makes us all better able to solve the problems and be more productive. In a world where even stepping away from our devices for a few moments is increasingly difficult, this level of sustained focus is undoubtedly valuable but also achingly challenging. The substantial achievements of my interviewees are the triumphs of purposeful curiosity. They've developed strategies to remain resilient and view mishaps as solvable puzzles rather than insurmountable roadblocks. Drawing on their journeys in this book, I bring together actionable, practical strategies and advice that anyone can employ to think like they do. I will repeatedly ask you to stop and think about what this all means for you and your life.

Although not everyone aspires to explore Antarctica, go to Mars, or invent a groundbreaking new product, we all search for meaning and we strive for progress in our daily lives. Purposeful curiosity comes into play in many aspects of life. You might simply be trying to become better at what you do, or you might be preparing for a new job—leaving your current career and pursuing something more fulfilling. Maybe you are trying to see through the noise of fake news or make sense of an information overload. Or you might be trying to commercialize an innovation, improve your health, or teach your children the value of solving a puzzle. No matter what you are doing, you can benefit from thinking like a purposefully curious person. My thesis is that at its core, a curiosity project can bring rich rewards, whatever your purpose. There are exciting mysteries to solve everywhere, but focused exploration is much more inclusive and accessible.

My goal is to make purposeful curiosity the new normal. Consider this book a master class in curiosity. Driven by an internal desire to become much better at it myself and learn anything I can to leverage its transformative power, I started researching everything I possibly could about curiosity. As a field researcher, I dove deep into this topic over the last eight years to uncover its inner workings. I immersed myself in academic studies, articles, and reports having to do with psychology, science, culture, and innovation. I talked to more than sixty people from many walks of life and professions to understand their purposeful curiosity journeys, and I consulted leading experts. Fortunately, success leaves clues. Among them are space and polar explorers, investigative journalists, entrepreneurs, investors, creatives, innovators, engineers, scientists, educators, and athletes (see the appendix for the detailed list of interviews). When I was compiling this list, I searched for people who exhibit a consistently pioneering spirit, who use their curiosity for creative problem-solving.

This book offers the tools to replicate their successful journeys. Each chapter covers a building block:

1. **Uncover your itch to know:** We can learn to find an itch and cultivate it. By focusing on a purpose that gets us up in the morning, and with a conviction that everything is understandable, we can transform any possible interest into an insatiable itch that drives our passion and fuels our perseverance.

2. **Go down the rabbit hole:** Our curiosity turns into a formal project when we share our excitement with others and allow ourselves to take ownership by investing time, energy, and resources.

3. **Conquer your fears with curiosity:** To conquer your fears, first, focus on partly muting the external world. Second, turn your curiosity inward to defeat your inner critic and explore who you are meant to be. Third, reframe your fears into impossible riddles, future regrets, and small experiments. Finally, turn your fear into something that becomes second nature to you.

4. **Become an expert—fast:** The best way to learn about our new shiny object is by creating our personalized curriculum and tapping into the knowledge of the community. We must listen and absorb as much as we can.

5. **Ask, "Who's with me?"** You must assemble the dream team. This is about hiring people who fit the CURIOUS acronym: They are *collaborative*, *unabashedly* passionate about the subject, *resilient*, and *iconoclastic*. They are also interested in *outside* issues beyond their area of expertise, feel an *urgency* to act, and *seek* surprises.

6. **Get ready:** To optimize your curiosity journeys, identify all the things that can go wrong and try to mitigate them methodically.

7. **Leap into the unknown:** To enhance our curiosity journeys, we must learn to set boundaries and prioritize. We must direct our experiences with all our senses and build a rhythm by breaking down the journey into manageable steps. We may also need to create our own tools if they do not exist. And finally, we must take corrective actions when they are needed.

8. **Develop resilience in the face of adversity:** To overcome setbacks and build resilience during our curiosity journeys, we need to remind ourselves of our purpose, reframing each setback as an opportunity to intentionally explore. We should create a strong support network and, fueled by positive emotions like excitement and interest, crack each mystery setback as a detective would.

9. **Turn the ending into your new beginning:** Reflecting on our completed curiosity projects, we must ask ourselves one crucial question: "Am I still curious to explore this field?" Depending on our answer, we can take one of two directions. Path A: We are still excited about our chosen field, and we have more shiny objects to explore further. Path B: We feel that we have exhausted this field, and we are keen to exit the current area and branch out to a curiosity journey in a new field.

As I said, reading this book and using its strategies for your own curiosity journey, new business venture, or research project will not make the strategies any easier. But they will become richer, deeper, and more meaningful. Think of this book as a curiosity manifesto and a practical manual designed to help individuals, teams, or organizations channel their curiosity to move ahead in their careers and lives, solve fascinating problems, and innovate. Through the curiosity journeys that I share, I want to change your beliefs about what is possible. I hope that the ambitious and groundbreaking challenges that my interviewees go after and their outstanding achievements will educate, motivate, and inspire a new generation of explorers and dreamers.

Curiosity should become the pursuit of many, not the privilege of the few. My goal is to encourage all of us to be purposefully curious and continue our natural lust for discovery. I want to help inspire a movement that awakens purposeful curiosity as the foundation of greatness and positive impact. I am personally invested in this cause, and I ask you to join me. The world needs us. Are you purposefully curious to find out more? Read on.

purposeful
curiosity

ONE

Uncover Your Itch to Know

> *The important thing is not to stop questioning.*
> *Curiosity has its own reasons for existing.*
>
> —ALBERT EINSTEIN

ON NOVEMBER 20, 2020, ROCKET LAB, A LEADING CALIFORNIA-BASED aerospace manufacturer, launched its Electron rocket, a small reusable rocket.[1] The launch was the brainchild of Peter Beck, an engineer from New Zealand and the founder and CEO of Rocket Lab. His longtime vision was to enable a variety of companies to use space travel technology to launch satellites that enhance a wide range of applications. These uses include more accurate weather predictions, high-speed global internet access, the ability to study other planets' atmospheres for possible life, the eventual transporting of goods, and, for more people—astronauts or not—the ability to experience space.[2] These challenges are typically addressed by government agencies like the National Aeronautics and Space Administration (NASA), but Beck felt confident he could tackle them without the cumbersome red tape of government, using the right lean, nimble team. Beck knew that the space industry could be disrupted if there was a cheaper way to get things into orbit. To do so, he had to figure out ways to bring down the cost of his rockets. While NASA's rockets can cost up to $1.6 billion to launch, each Rocket Lab small-satellite low-orbit (about five hundred kilometers) launch costs about $5 million.[3]

Beck assembled a team of engineers to develop a cost-effective, lightweight rocket he named Electron. At fifty-nine feet (eighteen meters) tall, the little rocket propelled small satellites into orbit.[4] The first Electron rocket was launched in 2017, and Rocket Lab had completed fifteen launches to space by the time the team decided to focus on the "Return to Sender" mission. This mission had two goals: to deploy thirty satellites into a circular orbit for a wide range of clients (commercial firms, academic institutions, research and development organizations, and government agencies) and to complete a guided reentry of Electron's booster into earth's atmosphere in one piece. The booster, the lower portion and the most expensive part of the rocket (the so-called first stage), takes the payload from the ground to space.[5] Because the boosters could be recovered in good condition while being subjected to intense pressure and heat when reentering earth's atmosphere, Rocket Lab could reuse them. This meant that the company could increase its rocket production rate and potential launch frequency and could vastly decrease the cost of getting to orbit.[6]

Before the build could take place, however, Beck spent significant time understanding what he needed to know to meet his goals. Curiosity was a key part of Beck's work. He had to undergo a great deal of learning and exploration to get on the right path. He told me, "If you don't understand all the challenges and opportunities around what you're trying to achieve, then you'll never reach a solution."[7]

Beck grew up in Invercargill, New Zealand. When Beck was a boy, his father would take him outside after sunset, where they would gaze at the stars in the sky. This experience led him to a boyhood fascination with space. "The fact that we don't know that much about what's up there, I just found that mind-blowing, and that hooked me," he said.[8] As time went on, his love for space, coupled with a passion for engineering, grew into an obsession and, eventually, a profession. He had a strong preference for building things from scratch rather than acquiring them ready-made off the shelf. Beck especially liked rockets. As a teenager, he became curious as to whether he could build one. He started by reading as much as he could about the subject and then began to experiment with different designs in his garden shed.[9] Finally, at the age of eighteen, he strapped a rocket engine to the back of a custom-made bicycle. Wearing a helmet and a jumpsuit, he climbed on the bike and, leaning his body forward, managed to ride at about a hundred miles an hour.[10]

Instead of attending university, Beck accepted a toolmaking apprenticeship at Fisher & Paykel, an appliance manufacturer, followed by a job at Industrial Research Ltd. (now Callaghan Innovation), an industrial research company. These jobs enabled him to learn while doing, let him hone his engineering skills, and provided him with access to machinery and material. Meanwhile, late at night, he continued to painstakingly work on and further develop his rocket engines. In 2006, Beck decided to take the

Without risks and the discomfort of newness that curiosity enables, there cannot be creative and intellectual breakthroughs.

plunge. He founded Rocket Lab to fulfill his childhood dream of building rockets.

Beck and his team at Rocket Lab managed to bring the costs of rockets down by using carbon composite materials, which are lighter and cheaper than metal. The team also built its engines using a three-dimensional (3D) printer to enable faster trial-and-error rocket development; this approach reduced delays every time a rocket engine blew up when early prototypes were tested.[11] Beck and the team explored alternative site options for their launches and eventually tracked down a remote sheep and cattle farm on New Zealand's North Island. There they could launch rockets more frequently because of the lack of other air or shipping travel in that region.[12] In August 2019, Beck announced his grand ambition to make the rocket's booster reusable. Up to that point, boosters were often abandoned after use mainly because they would break up during reentry into the earth's atmosphere and were therefore rendered useless.[13]

Electron's liftoff from the Rocket Lab launch complex on New Zealand's Māhia Peninsula at 02:20 UTC on November 20, 2020, was successful. Fifty seconds into the flight, the mission continued normally. Everyone in the mission's control center was anxious to see whether the booster would successfully reenter the earth's atmosphere in one piece and in good condition. Successful re-entry was not guaranteed in launches thus far. Beck quietly and confidently monitored the mission's progress on his screens. This was an important milestone for him and Rocket Lab; he had been preparing all his life to solve the mystery of the rocket's reentry. Approximately two and a half minutes after the launch of the Return to Sender mission, at an altitude of around eighty kilometers, or fifty miles, Electron's booster separated. Once the engines shut down on the booster, it began its descent. It hit about Mach 2 (around 1,290 miles per hour, or twice the speed of sound) before deploying three types of parachutes to reduce its speed.[14] This was the moment of truth. Rocket Lab technicians recovered the first stage of a rocket intact for the first time, fishing the booster out of the Pacific Ocean. Back at the mission control center, Beck was happy, like a giggling schoolboy.[15] His abundant curiosity and his task-minded work had paid off.

Rocket Lab had already made significant progress toward this goal even before the launch of Return to Sender. The company had guided boosters back to earth in a controlled fashion on two previous missions, but Return to Sender was the first time an Electron first stage came home under a parachute and was recovered after splashdown.[16] "The test was a complete success," Beck said during a press conference. "We're really confident now that Electron can become a reusable launch vehicle."[17] His vision was no longer just theoretical.

Space exploration is at the extreme end of the curiosity spectrum. Individuals like Beck personify the unique and far-reaching capabilities that we have for pushing our curiosity to the outer limits. Such journeys show us what we are all capable of when we engage the power of curiosity. They illustrate that the curious have a deep and persistent desire to know, something I believe all of us can develop and refine with practice.

WHY CURIOSITY MATTERS

Curiosity has long been the driving force of survival and progress. Across evolutionary time, curious animals were more likely to survive because they understood and adapted to their environments.[18] Throughout history, humans crossed borders and pushed into new territories to find a better place to live, to make a fortune, or simply to discover what was on the other side (sometimes with dire consequences for themselves or the inhabitants). Even during pandemics, we remain curious and continue to decipher complex mysteries. During the summer of 1665, a great plague broke out in London and beyond. Sixty miles away from the city center, the University of Cambridge temporarily closed. As a result, English mathematician Isaac Newton left the university where he had been studying and retreated to his family farm about sixty miles from Cambridge.[19] Isolated in this quiet yet serene environment and without any formal guidance from his professors, Newton used his curiosity to explore his interests uninterrupted.[20] He created new insights in mathematics and physics during this period and began shaping his most famous idea: universal gravitation.

Embracing purposeful curiosity allows us to discover whole new worlds. Without risks and the discomfort of newness, there can be no creative or intellectual breakthroughs. Curiosity is how we evolve, stretch ourselves, and make connections and discoveries that not only enrich our own lives but can change the world. Going outside our comfort zone via purposeful curiosity has a considerable upside. We can discover a whole new world, find our next inspiration, or meet a new thought partner. To push beyond what is known, we must break free from the everyday and ordinary.

UNEARTHING CURIOSITY JOURNEYS

Curiosity is the spark that ignites a chain reaction; it eventually enabled Beck's successful design of the Electron rocket. Everything around us—every item that we possess, every book on our shelves, every human connection we make—can be traced back to curiosity. Yet, unlike Beck, many of us struggle to identify a journey to commit to. For Beck, it was rockets from the time he was a small boy, and he applied himself with extreme vigor to his pursuit of excellence. For the rest of us, we are more likely to convince ourselves that we don't have the time and that even if we did, we wouldn't know where to start.

So, how do you ignite the spark? First, you need to get yourself into the right mindset. Then you need to look for inspiration. *Mindset* and *inspiration* are words we hear bandied about all the time. But we don't necessarily have a clear idea of what they actually mean, even less so how to achieve the right mindset or where to look for inspiration.

Mindset

To get into the right mindset, you need to make time, get comfortable with entertaining your own thoughts, and activate a sense of wonder. Let's look at each of these practices in more detail.

Make Time

As I have discussed, the modern world is designed to distract us, fracture our time, and steal our attention. Long working hours and the general noise of life—whether it's the actual sounds from the environment or the clatter of obligations—that permeates our daily existence have obscured what may be truly important. In this case, curiosity is the single essential puzzle that can motivate you to devote your energy and time to deeply engage with life.

One of the most significant barriers to curiosity is time. Let's be honest: It's never about *having* time; it's about *making* time. We have to deliberately set aside the necessary time to be curious about our world. The time we spend on our phones, browsing the internet, or watching TV could instead be used to start considering projects, to identify big problems, to discover our purpose, and to get a toehold on the mountain of understanding. Jólan van der Wiel, the award-winning Dutch designer whose personal fascination with extreme natural phenomena led him to conduct experiments with magnetism to shape and create objects, explained the importance of devoting uninterrupted time to your interest. "You really need time and space to think, to let it come in," he told me. "I definitely force myself to take an hour or two. . . . You can definitely force yourself to do that."[21]

Get Comfortable with Entertaining Your Own Thoughts

Once you've carved out time, you need to become comfortable within it. This is a really difficult task: How often do we pause time, particularly in the digital world that permeates our daily lives, and reflect on our thoughts? Research shows that pausing like this is challenging. A 2014 study published in *Science* found that people will go to great lengths to avoid boredom when they are deprived of other stimuli. Social psychology scholars from the University of Virginia and Harvard University asked individuals to put away their belongings, including cell phones and pens, sit alone in a room, and entertain themselves with their own thoughts for fifteen minutes.[22] Should the participants find the task too difficult, they had the option of distracting themselves by pushing a button, which gave them a harmless electrical shock. Across eleven separate studies, most people reported that they didn't enjoy being left alone to think. Two-thirds of men and a quarter of women would even choose to engage in an unpleasant activity (in this case, to knowingly electrocute themselves) at least once, just to alleviate their boredom.

My students and my seventeen-year-old daughter also fail to see the value in taking time to be entertained by their thoughts. I encourage them to see it as an integral part of purposeful curiosity since it breeds a generative mindset. Auriea Harvey, who over the course of any one day is a 3D artist creating sculptures, a professor of games, and a creator of video games, says she often visits her local cathedral in Ghent, Belgium, to just sit in stillness and engage with her thoughts. "This gets my psyche in order, kind of, and helps with focus and idea generation," she told me.[23]

Meditation, even the simple kind Harvey engages in, is helpful for problem-solving.[24] When we achieve the ability to be still in silence, we won't avoid being alone with ourselves—we will relish it and look for opportunities to practice it. Start by sitting down alone in your favorite space, or take a slow walk in a park, or even lie down in bed. Do whatever you can to reduce external stimuli. Although the lack of stimuli may feel uncomfortable initially, when you start to focus on your thoughts, the experience can surface interesting insights.

Activate a Sense of Wonder

If you look back through history, you will discover that many of the world's most curious minds didn't have just one single passion. Even if a person is so immersed in what they do, that doesn't mean they have no other interests in the periphery. We can be curious about more than one field, and multiple interests often lead to important new connections and discoveries. Einstein, the famed physicist, was a violinist and a fan of Mozart sonatas.[25] Da Vinci immersed himself into the fields of mathematics and engineering when he wasn't painting. Alexander Fleming, the Scottish physician and microbiologist best known for discovering penicillin, was a self-taught artist; he was a member of the Chelsea Arts Club, where he painted watercolors. Fleming also painted miniature houses, ballerinas, and soldiers using microbes.[26]

The curious never feel boxed in by what they do. They may love their day-to-day job, but there are likely to be a few things that they're keen on trying out. They get comfortable with what they know how to do, but they may want to explore as many new fields as humanly possible.

Several of the people whom I talked with described how reaching out to others in an emerging or rapidly developing area or exposure to the work or ideas of people outside their fields sparked their curiosity and opened up new areas of study. Angelo Vermeulen is one such person. An artist, a biologist, and a space systems researcher, he cofounded Space Ecologies Art and Design, an international transdisciplinary collective of artists, scientists, engineers, and activists. He has been collaborating with the European Space Agency's MELiSSA (Micro-Ecological Life Support System Alternative) program on biological life support for space for more than a decade. Currently, he works at Delft University of Technology, developing bio-inspired concepts for interstellar exploration, and together with the Leiden-Delft-Erasmus Universities Centre for Sustainability, he has been connecting space technology and horticulture to foster innovation in global food production. "I need this big sense of loosening up, of opening, of making the walls porous all the time," Vermeulen told me.[27]

Being purposely open to experiences and having an open and active mind leads us to unsolved mysteries and novel answers. You can start by opening up your interests beyond your professional field, taking up new hobbies, or attending talks in subjects that you know little about.

> *When we achieve the ability to be still in silence, we won't avoid being alone with ourselves—we will relish it and look for opportunities to practice it.*

Inspiration

Once you're in the right mindset, what do you need for inspiration? Inspiration may come from anywhere, but there are some concrete steps to aid your search. Initially, these steps may lead you to areas that do not interest you, but with time and dedication, exploration yields happy surprises and relevant discoveries. To get inspired, the preternaturally curious people I interviewed tend to ask five questions time and again:

- What if?
- Am I sure?
- What's next?
- Have I looked closely enough?
- Have I looked everywhere?

Let's ask these questions ourselves and go into a little more detail as we try to understand how they can help us become inspired.

What If?

Curious people use what-if questions to prompt new explorations and open up interesting possibilities. Jon Wiley joined Google in Mountain View, California, in 2006. His job was to lead the product design of Google's Search through the largest transition in its history: from desktop to mobile. Furthermore, Wiley had to build teams in new domains like augmented and virtual reality, and wearable computing. He drove the vision of ambient computing across Google for several years, with an emphasis on perception and wearable interfaces. Wiley explained to me that focusing on the what-ifs—always wondering, "What if the world were like this?" or "What if the world were like that?" or "What if I do that; what's going to happen?"—allows him to kick off new explorations and allows his curiosity to run free.[28] "I create my little science fictions," he said. "I tend to think about just a whole series of different worlds."[29]

Wiley is not the only one to use future-oriented scenarios to get their curious juices flowing. The last time I led a field trip with my students to Silicon Valley, we spent some time in the Institute for the Future (IFTF) in Palo Alto, California, a nonprofit think tank dedicated to helping people imagine future possibilities to make better decisions. Our guide to the future was Sean Ness, a director at IFTF. "Focus on the future of X," he told me after the trip.[30] "Explore different scenarios . . . ask questions that are relevant to that scenario: What's the best thing that could happen? What's the worst thing that can happen? How would my organization win in this future? What would we need to do to thrive or survive in that future? What kinds of skills do we need to hire? What kind of training do we need to give existing staff? What kinds of laws or regulations need to be changed to make that future happen?"[31]

Mary Katrantzou, the famous London-based fashion designer, similarly noted that she finds the creation of hypothetical scenarios with her team invaluable for meaningfully exploring fascinating new fashion concepts. "Sometimes we look at a certain topic and we put a theoretical scenario in place where the team looks at it from the eyes of a robot, or they look at it from the eyes of someone living a thousand years in the future," she told me.[32] This scenario-building approach ignites imagination and generates novel ideas.

Am I Sure?

Leading designer Michael Jager is the creative director and principal of Solidarity of Unbridled Labour, based in Burlington, Vermont. Jager, Vermont's first awarded AIGA Design Fellow, has been creating and collaborating with brands such as Burton Snowboards, Microsoft's Xbox, Nike, Levi's, MTV, Virgin, Lululemon Athletica, MasterClass, and Patagonia for more than twenty-five years. His TEDx talk "Saving Curiosity" focuses on how curiosity benefits our ideas, lives, and happiness.[33] Jager warns that curiosity is disappearing and discusses ways to reignite it in our daily lives. He told me that looking at patterns in our area of interest and understanding them is not enough.[34] Jager argued that creating magnetism that pulls people into an idea is all about "breaking pattern."[35] *Breaking pattern* is having the confidence to reject or put aside preconceived ideas and assumptions (patterns) and approach new things without judgment.

Jess Butcher, a London-based serial entrepreneur included in BBC's "100 Women" and *Fortune*'s "Top 10 Most Powerful Women Entrepreneurs," was appointed a Member of the Order of the British Empire (an MBE) for her services to digital technology and entrepreneurship in 2018. Intrigued by her entrepreneurial journey, I wanted to learn more about what triggers her curiosity. Butcher told me her eyes light up the moment she hears something that challenges her current thinking. "Oh, I'd never thought that before and I'd never heard that before, and that's unusual."[36] That's the point where the spark emerges. "Well, actually, I'm going to go and find out more about that because that's contra to my sense of the world or a worldview," she noted.

We all have ingrained beliefs and biases. Actively looking for or recognizing new information that challenges or completely disputes some of our deep assumptions or beliefs can trigger exploration. Challenge everything! Curiosity doesn't like rules; it is an act of protest.

Curious people believe that almost everything is subject to further exploration. They don't feel suppressed by knowledge; they question established orthodoxy. "If you're naturally curious," said Marshall Culpepper, an American serial entrepreneur in software, "you're going to find your way into the big problems pretty quickly, because you're going to traverse the landscape of things that people already know, through your curiosity, and then you're going to run into a trap. And when you run into that trap, you've found a thing that human envy still hasn't been able to figure out, and more, or importantly, those problems are the hardest problems that we face."[37] The challenge is to think about hard questions that few ask—and fewer answer. The curious are no strangers to challenging the status quo, and they sometimes do things that upset the rules of society.

What's Next?

Others ignite their curiosity by exploring what might come next in the technology world and imagining new and exciting paths. They understand that new frontiers hold potential, and they are eager to understand them. Wiley, the previously mentioned Google director, explained how his long-term interest in virtual reality, or VR (something that was always in his periphery from his university days at the University of Texas at Austin), got reignited. When his colleagues started working on Google Cardboard (the foldout cardboard that turns your phone into a VR handset), the potential of VR made him realize that people would interact with computers on a new, more personal level.

Many of my interviewees started experimenting with the internet when it first became publicly available in the 1990s. They then experimented with 3D printing or VR. Roberta Lucca's curiosity, for instance, piqued when she came across the 3D printing technology. Lucca is a self-confessed polymath (she is super curious and passionate about different domains). A serial entrepreneur, she started a jewelry company using 3D printing and founded an award-winning video games company in London. "I followed the evolution and science of 3D printing, including the impact it could have on the world," she explained. "I know quite a lot about how the fashion industry works and how wasteful it is. I thought, 'What if I designed and then created jewelry on demand?' I bought a 3D printer and started to create some jewelry."[38] Lucca saw that she could start a business that was also socially conscious. Realizing that she could design and then manufacture a bracelet in four hours in her home, she came up with the idea of creating jewelry on demand. "You wouldn't have 80 percent of the waste that you have when you have premanufactured products in stores that are never purchased, and eventually go into landfills," Lucca said.[39] Her realization marked the beginning of a curiosity journey to see if she could combine 3D printing and fashion to create an innovative and environmentally sensitive way to design and sell jewelry.

Have I Looked Closely Enough?

Daisy Jacobs, a British Academy Film Awards (BAFTA) winner and an Academy Award–nominated animator, suggests prolonged observation as a way of finding inspiration. She describes one such observational journey, done on her home's roof terrace. She would spend a few hours each time on her terrace and draw other people and what they were doing on their roof terraces.[40] This went on for about three weeks. "When you look at something over a sustained period of time, you start noticing details," she added.[41]

The time spent interacting in this way sparked several noteworthy observations that informed her animated short film work. Jacobs wasn't looking for surprises, but by simply observing over a prolonged period, she saw how different everyone was, how each person had their own way of interacting with their environment. When we force ourselves to observe familiar environments with a new focus, we are more likely to observe our surroundings in new ways. These observations can lead to new ideas. By spending time in the field, Jacobs observed several new patterns that immediately grabbed her attention.[42] One seemingly mundane observation project, like watching a roof terrace, would often transform into a three-week project. She noticed people putting their washing out or sunbathing; buildings came alive. When you are purposefully curious, you can often sit undistracted and observe and learn how things work. We can use curiosity to notice and truly appreciate what we are looking at. Prolonged observation slows us down and helps us be fully present.

Ed O'Brien, a social psychologist at the University of Chicago Booth School of Business, also found that recurring experiences like Jacobs's repeated observations were far more enjoyable than people expected them to be.[43] Why is this the case? Two of O'Brien's experiments suggest that experiences are not repeated exactly: Each time we rewatch a movie, revisit a museum, reread a book, or observe the same space, we notice new things, which in turn makes the experience at least partly novel. We must keep looking for novelty, searching for things that we didn't notice the first time. How can we exercise our observation skills? Go to a museum, visit a park, or attend a festival or talk. Force yourself to take a seat and observe what's happening around you. You can draw your observation in a sketchbook or take notes on your phone or a paper notepad.

Have I Looked Everywhere?

Through my conversations with the remarkably curious, what became apparent was the importance of being a contrarian. Curious people go right when everyone else goes left. They actively look for surprises. Playing the contrarian may be a difficult task for most of us, especially today, when there is a great deal of shaming on social media and in the traditional media. Concerns about fake news have bolstered a fear that anyone who is not an expert in an area has no right to do their own research or have an opinion about it. So, people often struggle to go against the grain and explore something new, for fear of ridicule. Empowered by their urge for discovery, curious people, on the contrary, are not afraid to go their own way.

George Kourounis, a Greek Canadian explorer, TV presenter, and storm chaser, is intrigued by some of nature's most extreme phenomena, like tornadoes, dust storms, hurricanes, avalanches, and volcanoes, and wanted to document them. He explained that extreme environments or weather conditions arouse his curiosity.[44] They drive him to find out why they happen, what creates them, and what makes them so powerful (and sometimes destructive). What he witnesses leaves him with a sense of wonder at their power and with many questions on what may be happening on other planets and whether life might exist elsewhere in our universe. Kourounis was the first person to make the descent into the Darvaza Crater, more commonly known as the Door to Hell, a giant 230-foot-wide flaming hole in the desert of northern Turkmenistan with mysterious origins. A popular theory suggests that in 1971, Soviet geologists set the sinkhole on fire to burn off methane gases but underestimated the gas reserves in the hole and that, consequently, it has burned continuously ever since.[45]

Wearing a heat-resistant suit and a self-contained breathing apparatus and using a custom-made climbing harness and fire-resistant ropes that would not melt under the extreme heat, Kourounis plunged into the flaming crater to collect soil samples at the bottom of this cavernous pit (temperatures can reach up to 400°C, or 752°F).[46] He was aiming to find organisms that survived this extreme environment. "We were looking for extremophile bacteria," he explained, "seeing if there's anything living in these conditions—hot, methane-rich conditions—because that could give us clues as to where we could look for life on other planets as well, because there are planets outside of our solar system that have similar environments. So, there was this larger goal, and so that was helping to drive me."[47] New questions emerged not only about the feasibility of the expedition itself but also about whether life could survive in such harsh conditions. The answers could shed light on whether life could survive similar conditions on other planets.

Exploration takes shape in many fields. John Fawcett is an American serial entrepreneur who was the cofounder and CEO of Quantopian, a company that aimed to create crowdsourced hedge funds by allowing freelance quantitative analysts to develop, test, and use trading algorithms to buy and sell securities.[48] Fawcett told me that Quantopian came to be when he explored the possibilities of combining crowdsourcing with open competitions and quantitative finance.[49] This arrangement hadn't been done in the past. "I had an overwhelming insatiable curiosity to know what was going to happen. . . . Once I thought of it, I just needed to know if it would work," Fawcett said.[50] Along with Jean Bredeche, Fawcett founded Quantopian in Boston in 2011 with the vision of making finance more open by providing software and an online community for securities traders to test their trading algorithms.

> *The challenge is to think about hard questions that few ask—and fewer answer.*

UNDERSTANDING THE ITCH EQUATION

You now know how to get into the right mindset and are armed with five questions that will open you to inspiration. The essential next step is to find a topic that interests you enough and that you can pursue deeply for a long time. When embarking on a curiosity journey, you have to feel passion for the topic of your choice and have confidence that it will sustain your interest. How do you know which journey is the right one? Why do people focus on specific curiosity journeys? What motivates them to focus on some topics or questions and not on others? In other words, why scratch this itch and not any other one? What makes this puzzle so seductive that people devote their curiosity for a prolonged period while the rest of us drift around various interests? For some people, it seems obvious. Remember Beck and his rockets at the beginning of this chapter? For him, his passion was always rockets. But there's no reason that you cannot begin a curiosity project at any time in your life and start from ground zero information-wise. But if that's the case—that you can spend your time fruitfully on anything—then how do you choose what to focus on?

Three components of a potential interest transform it into an insatiable itch that drives our passion and fuels our perseverance. For simplicity's sake, I like to put them together in the following equation:

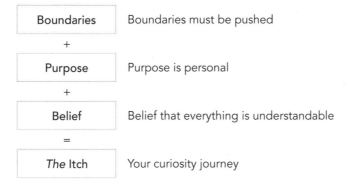

Boundaries	Boundaries must be pushed
+	
Purpose	Purpose is personal
+	
Belief	Belief that everything is understandable
=	
The Itch	Your curiosity journey

Let's look at this equation in more detail. What are boundaries, purpose, and belief? How can they be added together? And why do they add up to the itch—the project that drives your curiosity to the greatest heights?

Boundaries

What does pushing boundaries look like in practice? We can think about it in three ways. First, we'll want to address hard problems or seize exciting opportunities. Second, we identify an outer limit and aim to disprove that a boundary exists. That is, we go where no one has gone before. Finally, and bringing points one and two together, we'll look at how an audacious journey is fueled by something I term *micro-curiosities*. A big answer to a big question is made up of many smaller puzzles or mysteries. We might think of each of these micro-curiosities as a form of boundary pushing—with each small win representing a boundary broken on the way to a bigger goal. Now, let's look at these three practices in more detail.

1. Focus on Hard Problems or Exciting Opportunities

Curiosity focuses attention on addressing hard and interesting problems or seizing exciting new opportunities. This spark of interest is not surprising, according to Paul Silvia of the University of North Carolina at Greensboro, a psychologist who specializes in the emotion of interest. His research experiments show that when we evaluate something as new, unexpected, or complex it tends to spark an interest.[51]

Sir Norman Foster is a Pritzker Prize–winning British architect. The Pritzker is equivalent to a Nobel Prize for architecture. His firm, Foster + Partners, in Battersea, London, spans architecture, engineering, and industrial design. Examples include Apple Park in Cupertino, California (the giant ring-shaped office complex); many Apple stores around the world; the Beijing Capital International Airport (the third-largest commercial airport); Hong Kong & Shanghai Bank's headquarters in Hong Kong; and 30 St Mary Axe in London (better known as the Gherkin). Lord Foster shared a hard problem that had been bothering him for some time: "One billion of humanity is living in a slum, which means that they don't have access to modern sanitation, to power or heating, lighting, cooking. They don't have clean water. This number may double by

2030, or treble by 2050. Nobody is considering this problem. . . . Architecture certainly doesn't."[52]

Lord Foster doesn't shy away from reality, which can sometimes be scary or uncomfortable. Instead, he chooses the difficult path and focuses on dreams rooted in reality. He seeks big problems and offers solutions. Big problems can lead to tangible results. They are hard, uncomfortable, and interesting enough to be worth answering.

Lord Foster's focus on a seemingly intractable problem, slum dwelling, has taken him, his team, and the Norman Foster Foundation (a nonprofit institution) to different parts of the world to meet with experts in solar power and in infrastructure that doesn't rely on soil (such as boats and airplanes). They also talked to government officials in countries where slums are prominent to learn more about legislation and land ownership, and they met with other influential people who shared Lord Foster's vision.[53] Lord Foster and his team are on a mission to explore as much as possible about these areas to help transform the lives of millions of people around the world. His dream is taking shape. In May 2018, the foundation joined forces with Tata Trusts (one of India's oldest philanthropic organizations), Omidyar Network (a philanthropic investment firm founded by eBay's founder, Pierre Omidyar), and the Cadasta Foundation (a nonprofit that seeks to advance global land and resource rights). The collaborative launched the Odisha Liveable Habitat Mission, which aims to transform all slums in the East Indian state of Odisha to habitats. With a completion target of 2023, the project is being implemented across all 114 urban areas in thirty districts of Odisha, making it the world's largest slum titling and upgrading program.[54]

2. Go Where No One Has Gone Before

In May 2017, Google DeepMind's AlphaGo program defeated the Go world champion. Go, considered one of the world's most complex games, is much more challenging for computers than chess is. Players take turns placing stones on a nineteen-by-nineteen grid, competing to take control of the most territory. I had read some of Google's breakthrough research on the game and was intrigued by the company's mission to help solve problems via artificial intelligence (AI). I spoke with Raia Hadsell, a senior research scientist at Google DeepMind. Hadsell leads a research team studying robotic navigation and lifelong learning about how Google determines which tech areas are worth pursuing.[55] Hadsell stressed the importance of going to places where no one has gone before—of diving into the unknown. "If you're in the middle of doing research in a well-known field," she said, "then the boundaries are already there. It's almost as if you're optimizing for small gains. Whereas if you're right at the front of things that have never been done before, such as artificial intelligence, there's so much that's unknown."[56] For Hadsell, what is worth chasing is what has never been done before.

So, aim to go where no one has gone before. Take a cue from polar explorers and adventurers who long to take journeys that past explorers have not tried. Raphaël Domjan, the Swiss eco-explorer who completed the first solar circumnavigation in the world and is now working on the first solar aircraft to fly to the stratosphere, told me that his itch was "to be the one who is opening doors that nobody has opened before."[57]

3. Leverage Micro-curiosities

It's great to channel our curiosity toward solving a big problem, seizing an emerging opportunity, or exploring the unknown. However, big problems can be overwhelming. So while it can be motivating and energizing to shoot for the moon, we have to be pragmatic. Big journeys are not reached by a single dive into the abyss. They are made up of many smaller journeys fueled by micro-curiosities, that is, small puzzles, mysteries, or challenges that are inside our comfort zone and that motivate us to explore our domain of interest. By breaking down an ambitious exploration into smaller, more achievable bits, we come closer to our destination. The solution is to start with something achievable.

Auriea Harvey told me that she finds micro-curiosities throughout her projects.[58] Think of it as playing a challenging video game. At each level, we encounter new information and new micro-challenges or puzzles. These inspire a sense of wonder about the environments that we are in. Every time we solve a new micro-challenge, we move to the next level. Usually, the information or scenarios at the new level may become more complex. We may have to spend more time understanding them. Our curiosity is piqued. We develop a desire to learn more about what the next micro-puzzle will be. We continue exploring new micro-worlds, level after level. Without realizing it, our boundaries are stretched, our confidence is gradually built, and we get closer to completing the game.

When I started thinking about writing this book, I broke my research down into several smaller questions. My first micro-puzzle was to figure out a series of thought-provoking questions to ask people who had reached a high level of success through curiosity. When I eventually had the initial interview questions ready, my next challenge was to determine whom to talk to. Next came the challenge of reaching out to these people, interviewing them, analyzing their insights, and identifying commonalities or patterns in what they were saying.

Purpose

Purpose is a catalyst; it keeps you motivated even when you are struggling or facing mounting problems. The emotional connection to a personally meaningful cause or pursuit makes immersion natural. Everyone I talked with possessed an astonishing sense of a higher purpose: a pressing raison d'être. Purpose moves them toward their goals, helping them stay on course and persevere even in the face of obstacles.

Purpose was the driving force behind the Data Science Bowl, the world's premier competition for data science used for social good. Booz Allen Hamilton, a US-based management and technology consulting firm, partnered with Kaggle, the leading online community for data science competitions (with over one million members around the world), on a mission to bring together data scientists, technologists, other experts, and organizations to tackle big problems. The 2016 challenge asked the participants to create an algorithm to automate a heart function assessment process.[59] Teams worked on algorithms that could accomplish a manual and slow process that is normally carried out by cardiologists.

Typically, doctors take around twenty minutes on an MRI to assess a patient's heart function. The algorithms would analyze the images much faster.[60] Everybody was anticipating that the competition would be won by data scientist experts with a background in medicine. In March 2016, when the winners were announced, the results were unexpected. Tencia Lee and Qi Liu, two hedge fund traders who had never previously worked on neural networks, nor as a team, were the winners. They were the ones who came up with an algorithm that diagnoses heart disease from MRI images. Lee and Liu triumphed over nearly eleven hundred teams from around the world. They beat ninety-three hundred submissions in one of the most ambitious AI competitions ever staged.[61] Lee and Liu had spent all their spare time during evenings and weekends building and testing algorithms.

I reached out to Lee to learn more about how her guided exploration led to this breakthrough and why she had become interested in this competition in the first place. She told me how her curiosity had been piqued when she learned about this unsolved puzzle in medicine. She had wanted to make a difference: The possibility of coming up with an algorithm that could save people's lives was meaningful to her.[62] Lee and Liu's algorithm is currently going through all the testing and regulatory processes before it can be adopted, but if all goes well, Lee will have achieved her aim: she's a lifesaver.

We can also harness curiosity to better understand how to combine commercial reality with important causes. Martin Frost is a serial entrepreneur of technology and life science businesses like CMR Surgical. This surgical robotics company, based in Cambridge, England, aims to help millions of people around the world get minimal-access surgery. He explained how his purpose strengthened his inquiry into the robotics domain.[63] Frost's calling is to launch products that can change the lives of millions of people.[64] Vern Brownell, the former CEO of D-Wave Systems, a Canadian developer of commercially available quantum computers used by Google and NASA, is similarly driven to solve big, existential, impactful problems like curing cancer or dealing with climate change.[65] Frost and Brownell want to have as much impact on the world as possible—to foster change in a positive, lasting way. Their purposeful curiosity enables them to create value for society.

Belief

The last component of the itch equation is the belief that everything is understandable or will eventually become understandable with the help of others. It's a belief not in your intelligence but in your ability to learn and understand. When I was flirting with the idea of writing a book on curiosity, I was initially nervous. I have written a lot in my academic career but never on curiosity. This topic was new to me. Yet my belief that I could learn about and understand the subject gave me the confidence to take the leap of faith and launch this project. I had learned about other new-to-me subjects. Why not this one, too?

When people deal with a new, unexpected, or complex event, they have to assess whether they have the knowledge, skills, and abilities to handle it. Building on existing knowledge creates a protective comfort shield to get a curiosity project started; it inspires confidence to go beyond traveled terrain and create your own path. Scientific studies have shown that people tend to be interested in tasks that are new but that they somehow regard as comprehensible.[66] For instance, people tend to find abstract poems more interesting when they receive a hint that enables them to understand the verses.[67]

Tencia Lee, one of the previously mentioned Data Science Bowl winners, explained that machine learning was a difficult area but nevertheless one that she could see herself exploring. Lee often reads high-level articles in a range of fields, but if she delves deeper into a field, it usually has to be one that she is relatively close to and is somewhat familiar with and one that she believes she could add value to. "I do like to read high-level articles about just about anything," she told me. "But in order to really investigate the details and try to know an area very deeply, it usually has to be an area that makes sense to me already. Machine learning is an area that isn't easy exactly, but I was able to see myself learning, understanding it, and making progress."[68]

Curiosity can also help us move between domains. Vermeulen, the Belgian space systems researcher, biologist, and artist, explained how he transcends domains: "You have to feed curiosity from the belief that everything is understandable. It might take a couple of years, but you have to just let go of this idea that some things are not understandable. It's all, to a certain level, understandable. There is no magic, mysterious forces at play that enable only just a few people to understand something. I studied biology, so I can understand other scientific fields, for example."[69]

FINDING YOUR ITCH

Many of you may already have a clear idea of where your passions and interests lie. Some of you may be less confident. Yet we all have something, probably more than one thing, that makes us happy, sparks our interest, and consistently engages our curiosity. That is where you should start when embarking on a curiosity journey, using the questions and insights I've outlined here. Find a space that's comfortable and quiet, close your eyes, and daydream. Enter an uncharted territory where there are no manuals or rule books to follow. Keep a notebook next to you to jot down ideas as they come (alternatively, you can use the notes feature on your smartphone). Be as creative and imaginative as you can be; don't worry about grammar and spelling. Be specific. If you have done this exercise in the past, find your dusty notebook, review your ideas, and see which ones reignite your curiosity.

Use what you have learned about expanding on a question to begin your curiosity journey. In the chapters that follow, we will continue to explore curiosity using research from psychology, neuroscience, and management to further illuminate the purposefully curious approach to innovation and exploration. When you learn how to think with purposeful curiosity, you won't just change the way you view the world; you'll be empowered to change the world itself.

– THE TAKEAWAYS –

- The good news is that you can learn to find your itch and cultivate it.
- To unearth your possible curiosity journeys, you need to take these steps:
  - » Get into the right mindset. Among other things, you should make time for curiosity, become comfortable with entertaining your own thoughts, and activate a sense of wonder.
  - » Then look for inspiration by asking the following questions: What if? Am I sure? What's next? Have I looked closely enough? Have I looked everywhere?

- How do you know which curiosity journey to follow? Three components of an itch make it worth focusing on: boundaries, purpose, and belief.
  - » Pushing boundaries is about addressing hard problems, seizing exciting opportunities, or going where no one has gone before. Your audacious journeys are fueled by micro-curiosities, that is, lots and lots of smaller puzzles or mysteries.
  - » Purpose must be personal. Be emotionally connected to a worthwhile cause, and immerse yourself in it.
  - » Belief must be concrete. As a point of departure, believe that everything is understandable (or will eventually become understandable with the help of others).

- Remember that this filtering process is time-consuming and elaborate. So, take your time and enjoy the process.

TWO

Go Down the Rabbit Hole: Habits of Curious People

> *You see things; and you say, "Why?" But I dream things that never were; and I say, "Why not?"*
> —George Bernard Shaw, *Back to Methuselah*

Committing to a dream is always difficult. Launching a curiosity journey requires us to invest time, energy, and resources. It requires us to be brave. Yet taking active steps toward a dream is far more satisfying—not to mention more effective—than opting to wait and see. The curious people that I have talked to embrace a zest for life. Instead of focusing on why, they typically argue, "Why not?"

Hedy Lamarr was one of the most popular Hollywood actors of her day. Considered the most beautiful woman in films at the age of seventeen, Lamarr dropped out of high school to star in her first film, *Geld auf der Strase*, a German production. Lamarr continued her film career by working on both German and Czechoslovakian films. The 1932 German film *Exstase* brought her to the attention of

Hollywood producers, and she soon signed a contract with MGM and moved to the United States. Yet, until recently, many of us did not know that Lamarr was also a pioneering inventor. Her interest in invention began when she was five years old, when she took apart and reassembled a music box.[1] After that, she never abandoned her curiosity.

Although she was making major films in Hollywood, Lamarr was never satisfied with acting alone. She would work on inventions between takes, on set, and she had an inventing table in her house. During World War II, Lamarr dated billionaire Howard Hughes, an innovator on a mission to push the limits of engineering and safety to achieve aviation breakthroughs for the war effort. Inspired by his vision, Lamarr studied fish and birds and explored the fastest of each. From her studies, she drew a new wing design for planes by combining the wings of the fastest bird with the fins of the fastest fish. On showing the design to Hughes, he said to Lamarr, "You're a genius."[2]

Lamarr's curiosity led to continuous experiments. Perhaps her greatest breakthrough came in the early years of World War II while she was trying to invent a device to block enemy ships from jamming torpedo guidance signals. Lamarr and her friend, composer George Antheil, enjoyed long conversations about tinkering and inventing. Antheil recalled, "We began talking about the war, which, in the late summer of 1940, was looking most extremely bleak. Hedy said that she did not feel very comfortable sitting in Hollywood making lots of money when the world was in such a state. She said that she knew a good deal about munitions and various secret weapons . . . and that she was thinking seriously of quitting MGM and going to Washington, DC, to offer her services to the newly established National Inventors Council."[3]

Instead, Lamarr remained in Hollywood and channeled her curiosity into a worthwhile purpose: preventing the Germans from decoding messages. No one knows what prompted Lamarr to focus on this problem, but Antheil revealed that her design enabled him to create a practical model. In June 1941, Lamarr and Antheil submitted their patent application for a "Secret Communication System," and in August 1942, they received their patent. The idea was ingenious. Their patent used eighty-eight channels, a nod to the number of keys on the piano. Instead of being broadcast over a single channel, messages would jump, seemingly at random, across many channels in a process known as *frequency hopping*. If both the sender and the receiver knew in advance which channels would be used, a message could be easily decoded. But to a spy without the correct combination, the message remained indecipherable.

While US Navy engineers rejected Lamarr's invention as too complex, her patent served as inspiration for other product concepts.[4] In the 1950s, engineers from Sylvania Electronics Systems Division started looking at the ideas behind the Lamarr-Antheil patent. By the early 1960s, Sylvania implemented frequency hopping—not with the bulky mechanical apparatus described in the patent, but with transistors. The innovation was first put to real use during the US naval blockade of Cuba in 1962.[5]

The wide-ranging impact of Lamarr's invention was not truly understood until many decades later, when Lamarr and Antheil's groundbreaking work in frequency hopping gave rise to many other applications of spectrum communications technology such as Wi-Fi, GPS, and Bluetooth. In 1997, Lamarr and Antheil received two awards for their contributions to communications technology: the Electronic Frontier Foundation's Pioneer Award and the BULBIE Gnass Spirit of Achievement Award, making Lamarr the first woman to receive what is otherwise known as one of the "Oscars of inventing."[6]

When we revisit the past, we discover many individuals like Lamarr who, by taking ownership of a problem or an opportunity and devoting their time to it, turn their interests into curiosity projects. Like Lamarr, you may now have realized the specific and meaningful mystery you want to solve or the new area you want to explore. You have found your passion by listening to your inner voice and ignoring the noise around you telling you what you should do instead.

> *To get psyched about your curiosity project, you must become the protagonist of your own story.*

AND THEN WHAT?

Then you have to make it happen. Somehow, to scratch the irresistible itch that you have identified, you need to turn the initial Google queries and conversations into the first step. To make the leap down the rabbit hole, you must take several steps:

Get psyched about your curiosity project.
Grant yourself permission to explore.
Declare your interest to the world.
Hand yourself over to your curiosity.

GET PSYCHED ABOUT YOUR CURIOSITY PROJECT

Procrastination is anathema to curiosity. Doing nothing is not an option if your aim is to embark on a curiosity journey. The inspirational people with whom I have talked have one big concern: inertia—not following through. They argue that we must become unapologetically psyched about our curiosity projects and that the only way to convert an itch into a project is by motivating ourselves. We need to be hyped up if we're going to make things happen. There are three ways to get yourself psyched about a project:

- Put yourself in the driver's seat.
- Realize that it is now or never.
- Focus on positive possibilities.

Just doing one of these things may be enough, but why not do all three?

Put Yourself in the Driver's Seat

To get psyched about your curiosity project, you must become the protagonist of your own story. Every compelling curiosity journey has a main character. This character is you, and you may have a difficult road ahead. Donald "Don" Wilson, founder and CEO of Chicago-based DRW Holdings, one of the most successful trading and investing firms in the world, put himself in the driver's seat when, in the first decade of the twenty-first century, unstable financial markets caused many firms, including DRW, to lose money. Rather than let his losses defeat him, Wilson chose to redefine the setback as an opportunity and to turn the losses into problems he could solve.[7] With this approach, he developed a new framework for risk management systems and valuation sheets. "We were able to make all the money back that we had lost in a very short period of time," Wilson told me, "and dominate the liquidity in the pit during that period, because everybody else was kind of shocked and couldn't deal with it."[8] By taking control of his situation—by putting himself in the driver's seat—he put his curiosity to work.

WRITE A ONE-PAGE STORY. NAME THE PROBLEM YOU want to solve or the world you seek to explore. Explain why you should care about this or why this journey is so hard. Finally, show how you see yourself setting this in motion. Make yourself the protagonist of the story. Use this story to think about the first steps or actions you would take to get started.

Realize That It Is Now or Never

Getting psyched about a curiosity project requires a sense of urgency. You need to tap into your sense of yearning to explore what you find meaningful, and you must remind yourself that this is a time-limited quest. You only live once, after all. When others say, "It cannot be done," the curious respond, "If we start now, we might be able to do it."

Anand Anandkumar was at the peak of his career running a computer chip design company in India and China when he was diagnosed with cancer.[9] The news hit him like a punch to the face. Fighting and surviving cancer is a physical, mental, and emotional feat, and Anandkumar has seen this struggle up close—twice. His illness served as a reminder that he had better do something worthwhile. Anandkumar spoke of his mindset: "Do I just want a job and a life, or do I want to make a life, use the remaining time that I have to do something huge of value? My curiosity is only driven by an end goal of making a difference to human health. When I fell sick in my thirties, the mission of my life was to make a difference to human health. I knew nothing about human health, but I have a great opportunity to study for the rest of my life, and adapt."[10]

Battling his illness marked a critical period of self-reflection for Anandkumar, prompting him to question his life and work. This self-questioning had a massive impact on him. He realized that he wanted to stop moving from one opportunity to another. Instead, the time was ripe to get personally involved in something extraordinary, to address a big challenge the world is facing today. "And I sat on that for a year," he said. "That changed my complete outlook to say, 'I don't care about anything else. I will work on cancer.'"[11]

Equipped with renewed energy, he felt that he had to commit to this project immediately because there might not be another chance to do it. Anandkumar became the cofounder and CEO of Cellworks, a company specializing in personalized oncotherapy made possible by mathematical modeling frameworks. In 2014, he spun off Bugworks Research, a deep science start-up that aims to discover drugs to treat antibiotic-resistant bacterial infections. The company has won many national and international innovation awards and is the first company outside North America and Europe to win the coveted CARB-X grant (so named for its mission of combating antibiotic-resistant bacteria). Anandkumar, like other people driven by the curiosity itch, took matters into his own hands, created a sense of urgency, and committed to a curiosity project.

████████████████ **TRY THIS** ████████████████

WRITE DOWN HOW OLD YOU ARE. ASSUME YOU SPEND one hour per day on your curiosity project. Estimating that you will be productive until you are seventy, calculate the number of hours this schedule will give you. Now recalculate, using only one hour every other day. Over a long period, like your life, you are losing an enormous amount of time! When you look back at seventy, what will you remember? The hours that you did not spend on your project, or the hours that you did?

———

Focus on Positive Possibilities

Focusing on positive possibilities can also help us get psyched about our curiosity projects. The curious people whom I have talked to say, "I can make that better"—whatever "that" may be. Scientific studies have shown that people who focus on aspirations and accomplishments when they pursue goals—people with a *promotion focus*—are more likely to act than are those who seek to avoid losses. This latter group—those with a *prevention focus*—thus remain cautious and vigilant.[12] Framing your curiosity project positively is about enabling a desirable outcome rather than avoiding an undesirable outcome. The rhetoric of curious people emphasizes gains, and their stories exhibit a strong preference for action, movement, and eagerness over cautiousness and vigilance. They used words like *gain, benefit, win, advance, learn, care,* and *excite* rather than *avoid, lose, fail, waste, danger,* or *prevent* when they describe how they envisage the future. Adopting this positive mindset creates the space to explore. You have to recognize that any move you make opens up new possibilities. Remember that you often have more control over your life than you typically think. Shed your old skin, loosen your grip on what you have been doing, and see where your curiosity journey takes you.

Brett Lovelady, founder and CEO of Astro Studios, an award-winning new product development consultancy based in

San Francisco, starts each new design process with one question: "What can we do to improve the human experience?" Lovelady contends, "If you start out with that question, I think it helps you look at every project and problem with a duty."[13]

Astro Studios takes a bold and ambitious stand on how design solutions can leave an indelible mark on global culture and improve lives. Its designers visualize how a project is going to look to infuse it with warm feelings and positive energy throughout. "If you're really good at certain things," Lovelady told me, "you tend to repeat those things. You have to be careful with design because it's too easy to settle for what you've done before. If you're not careful, your designs risk becoming cliché. You're not as curious. But then I think . . . I'll go back to our mission to make the world a better place . . . I think we look at things and go, 'OK. This is really good design. That's a really good solution, but what does the *world* need this project to be?' And so, we challenge ourselves with as much a . . . I think it's sort of a desire on one hand and almost a requirement to move the culture or the industry or the market or the experience forward."[14]

TRY THIS

ASK YOURSELF, "WHAT PART OF YOUR CURIOSITY project has the potential to affect other people positively?" Once you have that answer square in your head, you can pin it above your desk or in your studio to remind yourself that you are trying to change the world and that your work has real purpose. Changing the world does not necessarily mean curing cancer or some other enormous undertaking. For instance, as an author, I hope to make this book more readable and to get my message across more clearly. We all have a positive contribution to make to our world. Now is the time to start it.

———

Shed your old skin, loosen your grip on what you have been doing, and see where your curiosity journey takes you.

GRANT YOURSELF PERMISSION TO EXPLORE

You have fallen in love with your puzzle but wonder if you can pull it off. It is all too easy to think of the myriad issues that stop us from embarking on the journey. You may have caught yourself thinking about starting projects and jumping from idea to idea without making the actual leap into uncharted waters. You may have gotten sucked into searching online, following one thread after another without really thinking systematically. None of us is immune to this approach, but it is impossible to start a curiosity project if we explore haphazardly and butterfly-like. You must take control.

Take ownership of your curiosity dream project. There is no need for others to define what success will be. No need for somebody to commission your purpose. No need for encouragement or reassurance to pursue it. The uber-curious people whom I have talked with are decisive and fast-moving; they seldom sit around when they could be working toward their goals. If people pigeonhole you as a Hollywood actor (or whatever), it is their problem, not yours. We are often scared to be someone else. Afraid to take agency. We need to grant ourselves permission.

Gavin Turk was a key figure in the Young British Artists (YBAs) movement of the early 1990s.[15] Turk studied at Chelsea College of Arts before enrolling at the Royal College of Art. It was there that Turk achieved notoriety by leaving his whitewashed exhibition space empty. The space contained only one English Heritage blue plaque in the style of the plaques the English Heritage Trust places on historic sites commemorating his presence: "Gavin Turk worked here 1989–91." In response, Turk was denied a degree by the school, but his talent caught the eye of the celebrity collector Charles Saatchi and was included in several YBA exhibitions.[16] His playful questioning of the concept of art and the role of the artist provided a conceptual framework for his subsequent practice.

Turk's work reiterates this witty and skeptical take on the world. His sculptures feature painted bronze, waxwork, even rubbish.[17] These pieces have since been collected and exhibited by many major museums and galleries throughout the world. Turk's reaction to his critical acclaim and artistic fame is low-key: "I've just had this idea that there is an audience for my work and that I just awarded myself, you know, it's this sort of artistic license," he said. "Who *gives* anyone an artistic license? You just give yourself an artistic license that if you want it, you've got it."[18] Turk's creative spark is like the curiosity itch, and when he talks about it, you can see how what he says applies to curiosity: "I learned very early on that, actually, in terms of art and creativity, in a way everybody is creative, and everybody can have that license to be an artist. A lot of people feel like it's something that belongs to other people, and they choose to give up on that," he said. "I suppose I've just been able to hang on to it."[19] We all have to learn to give ourselves the permission to follow the path that appeals to us.

FIND A FREE TEMPLATE FOR AN AWARD OR A CERTIF-
icate. Then type these words: "This certifies that
I, _____ (type your name), give myself full
permission to become curious about _____
(add a brief sentence about the domain that
you want to explore)." Then date it, sign it, and
put it somewhere visible in your home or office.
There's your license to be curious!

DECLARE YOUR INTEREST TO THE WORLD

When you find something that you are passionately curious about,
rather than initiating it in private, go public. Going public with
your curiosity project, either orally or in writing, can give you the
momentum to go through with it. Talk to someone you respect,
and tell them about your long-term goals and how you intend to
achieve them.

Felicity Aston is a British polar explorer, an Antarctic scientist
turned author, a speaker, and an expedition leader. In 2012, she
became the first woman to ski alone across Antarctica. The journey
of almost 1,084 miles (1,744 kilometers) took fifty-nine days to
complete and gave her a place in the Guinness World Records.[20]
Aston maintains that if you announce to the world, "I am going to
do X, Y, and Z, it is quite difficult to back down from that."[21] She
believes that it is important to be public about what you are going
to do and when you will launch, even if you may not yet have
anything concrete, because it makes you accountable to someone.

Involving others gives you a greater incentive for engaging with
the project. You have committed to start it. Sharing your objective

with the right person(s) is key. In 2019, researchers from Ohio State University and Penn State University found that sharing a goal with someone you believe to have higher status than yourself leads to greater goal commitment and performance.[22] Find people you admire and respect to become your accountability buddies to keep you on track, to act as a sounding board for ideas, and to keep you motivated about the curiosity project that you are about to launch.

TRY THIS

ONCE YOU'VE GIVEN YOURSELF PERMISSION TO EX-plore an itch, announce it to someone that you look up to and ask them to check in with you about your progress every month or so. Simple!

HAND YOURSELF OVER TO YOUR CURIOSITY

How we surrender to curiosity varies. Some choose the slow-and-steady strategy. They start small. They begin by committing time and energy to the project—a clear way to say to themselves that they are doing this—test the waters, and gradually make the leap. It is a mistake to think that to start something great, the only option is to dive in headfirst. This is not necessarily true. You can dip your toes in and get accustomed to the water first.

Still, some people do dive in headfirst right from the get-go. They invest in themselves and their project and quickly walk away from what is no longer serving them. Neither way to start a project is inherently better than the other. But you must dedicate yourself to launch your curiosity project, even if you do so incrementally. You must get out there and dip your toes. The truth is that some of us do not want to risk it all or take a dramatic leap for the new shiny object that just grabbed our attention. This fear of risk is why many of us start small and prefer a slow-and-steady approach to exploring our itch. Here are some ways to help you dip your toes into your own area of curiosity.

Dip Your Toes

Do Some Research

Scratch the itch: learn more about the subject that grabbed your attention. You need not undertake formal studies for a degree; you can find much information in libraries, bookstores, and online. Read as much as you can from the domain that piques your interest. Turn to Google and social networks for information. You can also watch videos or take a few webinars for inspiration. These are low-cost or often no-cost ways to become familiar with the new area of curiosity. Create a folder in your computer for the interesting material you find. Take notes. This research is reassuringly simple, and if this naturally starts taking more of your time, it is a clear way to tell you that you are becoming an agent of your curiosity itch.

Join a Group

When you have your dream topic in mind but have yet to figure out the first step, engage with people who are already exploring something similar to your interest. Or, more broadly, connect with individuals who have managed to convert their itches into curiosity projects. Figure out how they started, and gather their reflections from this initial phase. Ask them to share their most practical lessons, and learn from their failures. Several of the curious people profiled in this book highlighted how early conversations with experts not only helped them start their journeys but also led to long-lasting relationships. They found it critical to talk to experienced people who had already been through a curiosity journey and could guide them. These people turned into mentors, investors, and coaches. They turned into an ongoing resource.

Ben Saunders, the youngest man to ski solo to the North Pole, dragging a four-hundred-pound sledge more than six hundred miles through Arctic conditions, sought out the advice of an expert.[23] "I've been very lucky," he told me. "I've met a lot of people that I used to look up to as idols and role models. One of the most important lessons for me was realizing that if you ask the right questions, people generally respond positively. Wisdom and experience are only really valuable if you can do something with them. I was very surprised early on by how willing my heroes were to share what they'd learned. When I was seventeen, I wrote a letter to Sir Ranulph Fiennes, a British explorer who holds several endurance records, including being the first person to completely cross Antarctica on foot. He was one of my heroes at the time and is now someone I stay in touch with. It's the same with Robert Swan, the first person to reach both poles on foot back in the 1980s. He became a friend and patron of my last expedition. That was a big lesson for me, that people we put on a pedestal are actually approachable and they're normally very willing to share their wisdom. There was definitely a lot of interaction with these idols along the way."[24]

TRY THIS

MAKE A LIST OF PEOPLE WHO ARE ALREADY EXPLOR-
ing something in the domain that interests you
or, more broadly, who have converted their
itches into curiosity projects. Reach out to them,
and see if they are willing to have a conversation
with you. Make a list of questions that will help
you understand what their journey was like, and

make sure that you leave the meeting with at least three key insights on how to get started.

_____

> *By gradually putting your heart and soul into it, your little experiment turns alive.*

Experiment

Gever Tulley, a successful computer scientist, noticed how children today lack the same kinds of opportunities that he had as a child growing up in the wilds of Northern California. "Parents would scold their children for simple outdoor activities such as climbing trees, something I look back on as formative in my own childhood," Tulley observed.[25] Overprotective parenting and how it deprived children of learning about the world nagged at him for quite some time. So he started searching for ways to give children what he experienced in his own childhood. During a dinner with his friends, who confirmed how big this problem was, Tulley stood up from his seat, leaned over the table, and committed publicly to do something about it.[26] Dissatisfied with existing solutions, he started his experiment: a summer camp. In 2005, Tulley founded the Tinkering School to help children solve real problems by building things, using real tools and real materials, and learning about themselves throughout the process.

The positive response from children and parents convinced Tulley that he had to do more in this area, to make education better. Sometimes it is the simple questions that generate the most profound answers. Tulley's vision was to create a school where pupils would be entirely responsible for shaping their own learning experience. In 2011, he founded the Brightworks School in San Francisco. Brightworks is different from conventional schools. Instead of following a structured, exam-focused curriculum led by teachers, children work independently or in teams on projects they develop by themselves, and there is a lack of screens in classes.[27] The school resembles a laboratory where students can test ideas, iterate them, and create prototypes. Tulley's initial five-minute Google query turned into a multiyear experiment.

Doing research on your subject, joining a group, and experimenting are straightforward, affordable, and undemanding ways to figure out whether your itch has the potential to become a project. Taking those first steps—research, talking with like-minded people, and experimenting—can work wonders. For some, their curiosity starts as a hobby; for others, it's a side project. The people who follow this path will soon be unable to hide their excitement about how their little hobby or side project slowly morphs into a passionate project. By gradually putting your heart and soul into it, you make your little experiment come alive. As Tulley says, "Every significant change in my life and in my career is a result of chasing a question, of giving myself over to that curiosity."

> *Sometimes it is the simple questions that generate the most profound answers.*

TRY THIS

SET A SMALL, SHORT-TERM GOAL, AND ACHIEVE IT. For instance, if you want to learn French, learn how to conjugate the verbs *être* and *avoir*.

Go All In!

Some curious people cannot bear to take the incremental approach. They find their itch so irresistible that it requires their immediate attention and undivided investment of their time and energy. They walk away from commitments that are no longer important to them and go straight down the rabbit hole. They have a strong desire to create their own path and to take immediate control of their destiny. Throughout their stories, one point stands out: Their itch becomes their calling. They have a deep yearning for obeying their curiosity. This is where they find solace. These people go all in; some of them see no other approach. Let's look at some ways people go all in.

Do What You Love

In 2005, Maximilian Büsser invested all his savings to launch MB&F, a high-end watch brand in Geneva, Switzerland. Büsser visited several retailers around the world with the drawing of his first watch piece. At that time, all he had was a drawing. His hope was that on the basis of this drawing, retailers would pay for orders two years before delivery and would buy into the brand. Büsser was not at all sure whether his plan would be successful, but he went all in anyway. "I think, today, fifteen years later, I would not have the courage to do what I did then," Büsser told me. "Because you had to be completely and utterly insane. I look back and ask, 'What was wrong with you?'"[28]

Büsser graduated with a master's degree in micro-technology engineering from École Polytechnique Fédérale de Lausanne. His lifelong love of horology and high-end watches led him to senior manager roles at Jaeger-LeCoultre, where he spent several years growing the company, and to becoming the youngest managing director of Harry Winston Rare Timepieces. During his time at

Harry Winston, Büsser transformed the company into a well-respected high-end watch brand. To do so, he had to partner with very talented independent watchmakers who created cutting-edge movements. "That was the first time that any brand in my industry recognized the person that actually created the movement for them. And by getting to know these independent entrepreneurs, I saw how they lived, I saw how they thought, and I remember thinking, 'I want to be these guys . . . these guys. . . . This is me—this is what I want to be,'" he explained. "I had been a very creative kid who'd become a marketer, but I was creating for other people. I was creating what I thought would sell. I was not creating what I believed in. I was not creating what I loved."[29]

Büsser's reflection, combined with his experience working with talented independent watchmakers on several timepieces, planted the seed for developing his own high-end watch brand. "It took me two, three years," he said. "I had the idea in the drawer, and I was in my beautiful big office at Harry Winston, and I would open the drawer and think, 'That's a nice idea,' and then I'd close the drawer and continue. And then I'd open the drawer, and then I'd close the drawer. And then, at some point, as I say, you fall in love."[30] Büsser fell in love with the idea of high-end watchmaking and went on to start his own business.

Büsser not only managed to convince retailers in 2005 to buy his watch but also went on to develop one of the most sought-after high-end watch brands in the world—"kinetic sculptures for the wrist," as watch enthusiasts refer to them. His watches start in the tens of thousands of dollars and quickly rise to the hundreds of thousands.

Seize the Moment

Marshall Culpepper, a serial entrepreneur, was reading a magazine article about a start-up that was trying to put Arduinos, an open-source electronics platform based on easy-to-use hardware and software, into space. The idea was to help high school and college students design, upload, and run their own space-based applications, games, and experiments in a live spacecraft and get real, tangible results from space. "It's pretty inspirational if you think about it," Culpepper told me. "The start-up had raised a little money on Kickstarter and was looking for help."[31] He seized the moment: "I dropped everything I was doing and reached out to offer my software platform background." Just like that, Culpepper was all in. Less than a year later, the start-up had sent three satellites to the International Space Station. Building on that success, he then went on to found KubOS, a US-based start-up that develops a secure, open-source platform for space-flight software.

TRY THIS

WRITE A SHORT BLOG POST ABOUT WHY YOU ARE going all in. Explain what triggered you to do so, what you felt while going all in, and what you envision your new chapter will look like.

SAY YES NOW

Allowing your curiosity to take over loosens the grip on your past. If you want to be curious, you can, and you can do it on your own terms. But you must turn your itch into a project, not just talk about yourself as being curious. You have to embark on your exploratory journey. If you want to be curious, go down the rabbit hole *now*, put yourself out there, and worry later about your fears or how others see you.

− THE TAKEAWAYS −

- Say yes to your curiosity project now, and deal with your fears later!
- Get psyched. It is all about motivating, hyping yourself to convert your itch into a project.
- Grant yourself permission to take ownership of your curiosity dream project. Don't wait for others to tell you what to do or confirm that it is OK to start.
- When you find something that you are passionately curious about, rather than initiating your exploration in private, go public. Declare it to the whole world!
- Start investing time, energy, and resources. Hand yourself over to your curiosity either gradually or by going all in.
- Your curiosity project should not feel like something that you *should* do. It must feel like a project that you *have* to do.

THREE

Conquer Your Fears with Curiosity

> Nothing in life is to be feared. It is only to be understood.
>
> —MARIE CURIE

FELICITY ASTON SET OFF ALONE ON SKIS FROM THE ROSS ICE SHELF, the largest floating sheet of ice attached to land in Antarctica, the world's southernmost continent.[1] Her goal was to reach the Hercules Inlet, located on the margin of the Ronne Ice Shelf, on the opposite coast of Antarctica.[2] To make this thousand-mile trip, Aston would pull two sleds (about 187 pounds, or 85 kilograms) loaded with enough food, stove fuel, and ski equipment to conquer the threats of the unforgiving polar environment over a sixty- to seventy-day journey. If she could cross this expanse, Aston would make history as the first woman ever to do so on her own.

Born and raised in Hildenborough, a small country village in western Kent, England, Aston would not have considered her later life as an explorer inevitable. "One of my school friends said to me years ago, 'Of all the people I knew at school, you were the least likely to be doing what you're doing.' At secondary school, I would hide in the locker room to get out of playing sports where I'd be sent out in the freezing cold of winter in gym shorts to muck around with hockey sticks. I hated all of that," Aston told me.[3] Despite her antipathy for high school sports, Aston's interest in the polar regions began quite early. The fact that there were no mountains, snow, or glaciers in her back garden sparked her curiosity for cold climates. "I was fascinated by other places, looking at maps, and wondering what was out there," she said. "The idea that there was a land that we could fill with our own imagination, our psyche, because it seems empty, filled me with excitement."[4]

Aston's love of exploring was finally cemented when she went on her first polar expedition to Greenland, at the age of nineteen. This trip was the beginning of a love affair with Antarctica. "As soon as I left university," she explained, "my first job was with the British Antarctic Survey, the United Kingdom's national polar research program, where I was sent to Antarctica. The standing contract then was for two and a half years."[5] The program's purpose is to conduct world-leading science and operations in the polar regions.[6] Returning to England from this first stint after thirty-nine months, Aston was hooked and immediately started organizing her own expeditions. She sought sponsors and secured funding for various expeditions, including a 360-mile race across Arctic Canada in 2005, an expedition to Siberia in 2007, and the 2009 Marathon des Sables, the six-day, 251-kilometer (156-mile) ultramarathon across the Sahara Desert.[7] Aston was driven by an urge to experience and explore these places and stretch her limits.[8] She completed all these treks successfully, but she wasn't done yet.

Despite all these challenging expeditions, Aston's experience in Antarctica stuck with her. "You get to see Antarctica on good days

*Starting a journey with an unclear
path and an unfamiliar destination
requires you to cede complete control.*

or bad days," she said. "And it's a tough act to follow. When you leave Antarctica, it's hard to find something, or it was for me. It was hard for me to find something that filled that same level of awe, fulfillment, and reward. The polar region became my primary focus."[9] Then, the idea of skiing alone across Antarctica piqued her curiosity. Aston started preparing for this exciting adventure. Among other measures, she researched and selected the right high-tech equipment to protect her from the elements, did physical training, and prepared mentally by seeking advice from a sports psychologist who specialized in aloneness.[10]

On November 25, 2011, a plane dropped Aston at the Ross Ice Shelf, one of the most remote regions on earth.[11] As the plane disappeared in the clouds and Aston set off on her journey, reality hit her hard. On the first day of the expedition, she felt terrified. The temperature was near −36°C (−33°F), and the wind was strong enough to lift her tent into the air, and of course, the crevasses, cracks in the ice that leave wide holes hundreds of feet deep, were often hidden beneath snow drifts and presented the most devastating danger.[12] She had to grapple with legitimate fear, quite intimately and quite frequently.

The fear had started pulling at her before the actual journey began. "I remember in the lead-up to the solo expedition, I'd wake up at night with sweaty palms, in terror, thinking about what could go wrong," Aston remembered.[13] There were valid reasons to be frightened. When her lighters stopped working during her expedition, she couldn't light her stove. Windstorms lowered her visibility to less than a hundred meters, and crossing crevasses often felt like a death sentence.[14]

How did she overcome her fears and become comfortable with taking what were genuine life-threatening risks? "There are many different strategies to overcome anxiety," Aston explained.[15] "Remind yourself of what you've accomplished in the past and how you felt about it, and use that to reassure yourself. Take the new adventure slowly and build on it to gain more confidence, and learn to accept the unexpected. Give up complete control, and make decisions as they occur." Using these tactics, Aston kept moving forward. Her approach worked, despite numerous challenges along the way. On January 22, 2012, she reached her destination at Hercules Inlet. She became the first woman to ski solo across Antarctica and the first person to ski alone across Antarctica using just muscle power, without kites, dogs, or machines. The 1,744-kilometer (1,084-mile) trip took her fifty-nine days and earned her a place in the Guinness World Records.[16]

FEAR ISN'T ALWAYS BAD

Not surprisingly, our brains are hardwired for worry. Fear can be a valuable tool; it can help us separate safe situations from dangerous ones. It encourages caution when caution is due. Our hunter-gatherer ancestors had to keep an eye out for life-threatening or other dangerous situations, including animal and human predators. When our lives are threatened, fear protects us. It gives our brain subtle feedback; it may clarify that something is important and nudge us onto the right path.

However, many fears are unfounded. We construct fears that, rather than offering us protection, can instead severely limit our ability to achieve personal or professional goals, experience happiness, or develop our lives meaningfully. They can keep us from achieving our dreams and living our best lives. They can keep us small because baseless worries shut down exploration, make our thinking more rigid, and drive neophobia, the fear of anything new.[17] Stressful situations trigger the release of the stress hormone cortisol, which interferes with neural growth. Prolonged stress impairs our ability to learn and maintain physical health.

A hindering fear almost always follows a what-if approach to anything new. To fully engage your curiosity, learn to distinguish between valid fears and unsubstantiated ones. For those who engage in life-threatening pursuits, much as Canadian adventurer and storm chaser George Kourounis does, curiosity itself can be the best way to overcome fear. "The opposite of fear is curiosity," he said. "If you're afraid of something, you try to distance yourself from it. If you're curious about something, you are magnetically drawn to it."[18]

COMMON CURIOSITY FEARS

Polish sociologist and philosopher Zygmunt Bauman defined fear as "the name we give to our uncertainty: to our ignorance of the threat and of what is to be done."[19] Like Aston, most of the people I talked with while researching this book faced fear. They were filled with self-doubt and trepidation around new ideas. They experienced one or all of the three fears that most often prevent curiosity projects from becoming fully realized: fear of the unknown, impostor syndrome, and fear of discovery or standing out.

Fear of the Unknown

Starting a journey with an unclear path and an unfamiliar destination requires you to cede complete control, because while you know where you are starting from, it's seldom clear how you will get here. Given that our aversion to the unknown is hardwired into us biologically, it is not unreasonable that we cling to the environments we know. But what fuels our fear of the unknown, what really hinders us, is our fear of failure. Aston's self-doubt about how well she had prepared for the psychological challenges of being alone in an empty, hostile landscape crept in during the planning stages of her expedition.[20]

The Impostor Syndrome

The impostor phenomenon, an idea originally codified by psychologists Pauline Clance and Suzanne Imes, refers to a pervasive feeling of self-doubt, insecurity, or fraudulence that persists even when a person exhibits overwhelming evident success.[21] Impostor syndrome has been known to strike after an especially notable success or accomplishment, like public acclaim or an award. For example, research shows that nearly 70 percent of people experience impostor syndrome. Even well-known, accomplished figures like David Bowie, Tom Hanks, Lady Gaga, and Serena Williams have often admitted feeling like an impostor.[22] The impostor fear may hit us early in our curiosity journeys, sometimes right from the get-go. We idolize people who achieve great success in areas we long to explore, but with admiration comes self-doubt. When we compare ourselves with people who have recognized accomplishments, we can take ourselves out of the running. We feel we have no right to compete or go after the same things those before us have reached

for. Venturing into a new project or field, no matter how successfully you managed previous projects and roles, could leave you
feeling like a fraud.

Fear of Discovery or Standing Out

We know that the best way to learn is by directly experiencing
something that pushes us out of our comfort zone. We also learn
through experience that when we try and fail, we can feel disap-
pointment, embarrassment, and even shame. Our mistakes are also
often policed or at least observed and judged by others. That's because pushing boundaries or having the audacity to try something
bold can be scary. People who disrupt industries or shift cultures
threaten the status quo and can make others uncomfortable. This is
why people who act on their curiosity are often regarded as weird
or quirky. Under threat of torture, Galileo recanted his proof that
the earth moved around the sun. We are strongly motivated to go
with the grain, not to upset the apple cart.

The curious people whom I talked with experienced other
people's judgment in different ways. Some said that people in
their networks tried to "protect them" by discouraging them to go
forward with projects they wanted to pursue, warning them of the
dangers of questioning the status quo. Other colleagues and asso-
ciates posed patronizing questions about the value of their ideas.
Fear of people's criticisms or judgments should not hold you back.

Kourounis stressed how he sees reality: "People are capable of a
lot more than they think they are, and they tend to hold back and
think, 'Oh, I could never do that,' or 'I'm not capable of doing that,
and I couldn't just drop everything and . . .'—whatever it is they're
interested in but are afraid to do. But, over and over again, I've
seen people do things that they never thought they were capable

of doing, and it's just a matter of trying. People are afraid to try, and . . . the cost of not trying outweighs the risk of being unsuccessful. Doing nothing is the absolute worst thing you can possibly do, because if you take the risk and you succeed, fantastic. If you take the risk and you fail, learn from it. If you do nothing, then you have neither succeeded nor learned. The danger of inaction far outweighs the risk of doing almost anything, really."[23]

FEARLESS CURIOSITY

The more I listened to the incredible curiosity journeys of the people I interviewed for this book, the more it became clear that these highly accomplished people used similar methods for conquering fears. All of them used what I now consider a five-point plan:

1. Mute the dream stealers. Filter the external noise. Focus on partly muting the external world.
2. Reframe your fears as questions, riddles, and experiments.
3. Look inward, and silence your inner critic.
4. Explore who you are meant to be.
5. Turn fear into your second nature; make it part of the curiosity journey.

Mute the Dream Stealers

The first thing successfully curious people do to address fear is turn the volume down on the outside world. They are certainly inspired by others, and while they may listen to advice from all corners, they don't necessarily heed all of it. Curious people declutter their minds of what's irrelevant, especially what other people say or think about their endeavors. People around us may feel uncomfortable when they hear about our new journeys, and they may project their fears on us just as parents who regularly subject their children, often sub-consciously, to their own fear-based thinking do.

Daisy Jacobs, the previously mentioned award-winning anima-tor, found out about stop-motion—using the camera and animat-ing with raw footage—during her postgraduate studies. "In 2D animation," she explained, "you go back and you edit and you refine images and you reanimate bits and you add layers. But in stop-motion, you take the photo and that's it. That's raw footage, and then you take the next one and that's it, and then you take the next one, and that is your bit of animation."[24] Stop-motion films are a labor-intensive process, and you might spend a whole year working on a short film (one that is less than ten minutes long). Throughout her studies and work, many challenged Jacobs's curi-osity in stop-motion: What are you going to do with that? How will you get a job? How will you make money?[25]

Our critics' projections are not about us. What they project is about them and how they see the world. They may tell you that your potential exploration is too difficult or unworthy. They may even say that you cannot do it, so why bother trying. By ignoring the dream stealers, Jacobs started working hard and fo-cused on her short stop-motion film *The Bigger Picture*, a story about two adult brothers who struggle to care for their aging mother and who fight but manage to see the bigger picture.[26] "I started experimenting with painting and stop-motion because I liked painting originally when I did illustration a long time ago I liked painting."[27] Being creatively engaged meant spending her days in a hangar doing very large paintings, animating characters or ob-jects, and building her own world. "It's almost like blocking out other things," she remarked. "I think it's like saying to yourself it's completely valid that I'm interested in this and that I'm going to spend a year on it."[28] Having faith in what you are interested in will tune out negativity.

Remember, we allow our dreams to be stolen. Comparing ourselves with the people around us can be dangerous but it's also nature at work. A classic study by Franciscus "Frans" de Waal at Emory University found that capuchin monkeys were perfectly happy exchanging their stones for cucumber slices until the monkey next to them started getting grapes. All of a sudden, the monkey that had received the cucumber slices refused the rewards, became agitated, and actively rejected its food.[29]

The capuchin monkeys' reactions echo our own behavior. As toddlers, we play happily with our toy until we see someone else playing with a shinier object. We compare grades at school and university. We compare salaries and job titles in the workplace. Today, we live in an era of extreme scrutiny and judgment. Some of us care about how many likes we receive on our social media accounts, and we can feel upset if somebody writes a negative comment. Some people manicure their media profiles, creating a perfect picture that makes the rest of us feel as if we can't compete.

In one study in Japan, Taishi Kawamoto, Mitsuhiro Ura, and Kazuo Hiraki surveyed five hundred twenty- to thirty-nine-year-olds about social rejection. The researchers found that curious participants (those who scored higher in the Curiosity and Exploration Inventory-II, a scale measuring one's degree of curiosity) were less likely to experience reductions in life satisfaction or increases in depression than their less curious peers were.[30] These results suggest that maintaining our curiosity may allow us to recover more quickly from social rejection, an experience that can often feel devastating. "Don't waste time worrying about what other people think about you," Büsser, the high-end horologist introduced previously, told me. "If you're scared of being wrong—which is the same thing as 'What will people think?' then you're in a prison. . . . 'What will people think?' has killed more dreams than failure ever will."[31]

In some business schools where I've taught, I remember being criticized for having a wider range of interests and research questions than the typical academic has. I've heard the following questions about my wider range of interests, often when I was trying to research something that wasn't in my area of expertise: "Don't you think it is better to stick to what you know?" I'd be asked. "Why do you want to explore this research question in this new field?" "Don't you realize that it does not fit your current research?" "Have you thought of the opportunity costs of going that way?" "It will take you years to publish something novel in this area! Are you making a foolish mistake?" There is indeed some validity to these statements, since exploration beyond one's expertise *is* a risk and can turn into a waste of time if not managed well. However, what many of my colleagues were underplaying was the importance of looking at what we don't know or understand; such examination is the underpinning of all good academic inquiry.

TRY THIS

THINK OF A NEW AREA, IDEA, OR TOPIC THAT YOU want to explore, and share it with a diverse range of people. Write down their concerns, their objections, and any problems they foresee with your idea. Choose a place at home or work where you feel comfortable and can block out everything external. Then repeat to yourself: "It is fine that I am interested in this." Start delving deeper into your new adventure by considering each concern that they shared with you. If the concerns are valid, address them. If they are not, delete them.

> *Maintaining our curiosity may*
> *allow us to recover more quickly*
> *from social rejection, an experience*
> *that can often feel devastating.*

Reframe Your Fears as Questions, Riddles, and Experiments

When you are purposefully curious, you can move forward more easily because curiosity itself allows you to change how you approach your fears around new interests. This practice is called *framing*, the ability to highlight the relevant aspects of a situation while excluding irrelevant details in assigning meaning to what you are doing.[32] Some reframe their fears as questions or riddles to be solved, an effective strategy that can make facing fears enjoyable. This technique provides a lens that enables you to work through and even thrive amid fear—it's a riddle or a code to be cracked, not something to be afraid of. John Fawcett, the previously mentioned serial entrepreneur and cofounder of Quantopian, explains that "if 99.9 percent of people can't solve the puzzle, then what's at risk? If [you] try it, then you're just kind of like everybody else who couldn't do it either, but if you try it and you succeed, then that's magnificent, and you did something that almost no one else could've done."[33]

Others reframe their fears of venturing into the unknown as experiments. Michael Robotham is an internationally recognized crime fiction writer. He has twice won the Crime Writers' Association Gold Dagger award for best novel and twice been short-listed for the Edgar Award for best novel.[34] Robotham was born in Australia and as an adult moved to London to pursue a career in journalism. He worked as a reporter and rose to become the deputy features editor of the *Mail on Sunday*. He loved journalism, but his childhood dream of becoming a full-time fiction writer never left him.[35] He decided to leave the *Mail on Sunday* and started freelancing for the *Sunday Times* and magazines.

At the same time, he started ghostwriting because he was curious to see whether he would have the discipline to work for a long period on a book.[36] Ghostwriting proved to be the next step for Robotham. He ghostwrote fifteen autobiographies of famous people in the arts, sports, politics, and military. In 1996, Robotham returned to Australia and continued writing.[37] In 2002, his first novel, *The Suspect*, triggered a bidding war at the London Book Fair and was ultimately translated into twenty-four languages. "It was sold all around the world on 117 pages," Robotham told me. "All these publishers bought this book based on 117 pages, and I couldn't tell them how the book ended, because I had no idea how the book's going to end."[38]

I asked him how his curiosity enabled him to be such a prolific author of crime novels. Robotham explained that he is magnetically drawn to the path less trodden because doing so will bring him a more interesting life. He deliberately reframes venturing into the unknown as experiments, which is how he looks at plot and character development. "In my latest book [the experiment] has been the point of view of a very troubled teenage girl, first-person narrative. That's an enormous challenge for a writer to inhabit the skin of not just another human being but someone that's not like me at all, and that's how I keep it interesting. It terrifies me, and if I'm terrified, then I know it's interesting. If I'm terrified of making a mistake and having people accuse me of getting it wrong, that's good because that will make me work very hard—very hard—to get it right," Robotham remarked.[39] He views his experiments as temporary instead of permanent. It is about the exploration and learning rather than the outcome itself.

WHAT FEAR DO YOU HAVE THAT YOU COULD RE-
frame as a question, a riddle, or an experiment?

Look Inward, and Silence Your Inner Critic

The word *curious* stems from the Latin *cura*, which means "care."
Fueled by interest and compassion, self-curiosity starts by replac-
ing your nasty inner voices with kinder ones.

ME: I will start this new research project on curiosity.
LITTLE VOICE: *What do you know about this topic? Nothing!*

ME: I'll learn as much as I can about it.
LITTLE VOICE: *Oh no you won't.*

ME: I also want to write a book about it.
LITTLE VOICE: *You? Write a book? Ha-ha-ha!*

Listening to our inner critic hinders our progress when it comes
to making the next move. Most of us never properly address our
concerns, and we allow our fears to hold back our ambitions.

Instead of accepting a terrible outcome as a predictable conclusion, investigate your fears more closely and rationally. Give yourself a compassionate pause, and then analyze the negative voices
in your head. Next, write down positive statements to help counter
those negative ideas. The best way to cancel a negative belief is
to develop its positive counterpart. Instead of saying, "I am afraid
of doing this because I may fail," look in the mirror and say to

yourself, "I am prepared for this. I am ready. If I fail, I will try again because failure at something new is not final. It's part of the process of reaching success."

For example, imagine that you are curious about running, but you have never done anything athletic. You turn up at your local running club for the first time, not knowing anyone and feeling as though everybody else will be better than you. Your mind begins its usual process of worry: "What if I can't keep up?" "What if I fail?" "What if the others feel I am a drain on their progress?" "What if they don't like me?" And so on. When these doubts arise, you can turn them around by flipping the script:

QUESTION: What if I can't keep up?
ANSWER: I will talk to the group leader and ask if the club has groups that run at different paces, so that I can run with others at a similar speed and level.

QUESTION: What if I fail?
ANSWER: What if I do? I probably will. So what? I will keep going. I'll try again. The more I do it, the better I'll get. Everyone in the group failed at some aspect of running when they started.

QUESTION: How can I incorporate myself into the group?
ANSWER: First, I will stay in the now and embrace the state of being a beginner. Second, I will focus on learning and improving. The most important thing is not my pace or when I finish but that I turned up. I am running and I will finish. Third, I see something positive in not being the best at the moment in my pace group. I feel really motivated to turn up again.

QUESTION: Am I right to be afraid?
ANSWER: Yes. I have never run before. But as fears go, it's a minor one. If there is something I need, the people in the group are supportive and will help.

███████████████ **TRY THIS** ███████████████

TRY SOMETHING NEW THAT PIQUES YOUR CURIOSITY. Take some deep breaths, and instead of giving in to worries, self-doubts, or accepting a terrible outcome as a predictable conclusion, investigate your fears more closely and rationally. Be self-curious, not self-critical, when you analyze the negative voices in your head. Next, write down positive statements to help cancel the negative beliefs.

The best way to cancel a negative belief is to develop its positive counterpart.

Explore Who You Are Meant to Be

Take a break from comparing yourself with others and silencing your inner critic to create space to explore your honest, authentic, and vulnerable self. Don't let the noise of others' opinions and your own negative thoughts drown out your own inner voice. Instead, turn the curiosity spotlight on yourself. Any exploration often feels like self-exploration. You must discover as much as you can about yourself to be able to counter your fears: find out what makes you unique, explore the potential gains, and stretch how far you can go. In this way, curiosity is a response to a mysterious inner calling.

What Makes You Unique

Roberta Lucca, whom we met in an earlier chapter, was born in Rio de Janeiro, Brazil. After studying computer science and earning an MBA in management and one in marketing, she worked in television for seven years in Brazil.[40] Intrigued by television companies' experimentation with different technologies to make the viewing experience more interactive, Lucca began thinking about the video game experience in a similar fashion. "Watching TV (or a movie) is very easy," Lucca explained. "You just sit and absorb. Games require you to think through, you need to do something before you get the reward." As an alternative to passive TV entertainment, Lucca got seduced by the potential for enjoyment in immersive video games. She left Brazil and moved to London to pursue her interest without a job or a support network—and barely speaking English.

Mixing her wide-range curiosity with her entrepreneurial flair led her to found or cofound several businesses, including Bossa Studios, the BAFTA-winning game developer and one of the most successful video game companies in Europe. Its games are played by millions of people around the globe. Lucca also launched a firm that sold 3D-printed jewelry on demand and an AI coaching app.

Lucca took time off from work to turn her curiosity inward, wanting to understand more about who she was and what made her unique. Being interested in different things and having a portfolio career as opposed to becoming an expert at just one thing triggered her self-discovery journey. She wanted to understand why she did what she did. Her introspection made her realize that she became bored when she tried to be a specialist. That was when she came across the term *multipotentialite*, which was coined by writer and artist

Emilie Wapnick to describe people who have a range of interests and creative pursuits over their lifetimes.[41] "When I discovered the idea of multipotentialite, I became more comfortable with myself," Lucca told me. Because she allowed her curiosity impulses to help her become a computer scientist turned entrepreneur, turned angel investor, turned influencer, turned public speaker, her voracious appetite for what's new, what's next, continues to expand.

TRY THIS

BECOMING CURIOUS ABOUT A NEW DOMAIN MAY make us insecure. We may not have the background or education in this sphere. We may feel like a fraud. But we can counteract this fear by becoming self-curious about our unique qualities. We should regularly ask ourselves *what*, *why*, *why not*, and *how* questions to understand why we behave the way we do and to get in touch with our inner world. Our goal should not be to try to become like the people who are already in this domain but rather to discover what new insight we can bring to it.

Be Curious About the Gains

There are huge upsides to pursuing curiosity journeys. Learning what interests us can lead to new opportunities, businesses, and experiences. These journeys are life enriching. We also learn more about ourselves, gain confidence, and become stronger and more resilient. Doing the same thing over and over again may make us more efficient, more successful, and possibly richer, and there's nothing wrong with any of these. Having a safe and comfortable life, though, may make us keep on course. Let me be cynical for a moment. It sounds silly to give up the security of a guaranteed paycheck or a career that we worked hard to nurture and may even love. I am not talking about walking away from something that you love just for the sake of change. If you like what you are doing and derive satisfaction from it, keep going.

However, we keep forgetting, sometimes consciously or sometimes subconsciously, that what ties us to no-longer-satisfactory situations is often not just inertia or procrastination. It is a way of seeing the world. Until we can let go of old, worn-out habits, security and routines may hold us prisoners. So, for many of us, it feels strange to shake up our safe and comfortable lives, even when we no longer find them fulfilling. In talking with people who practice purposeful curiosity, I've learned that they were able to move beyond stabilizing habits and mindsets. Some of these people, for instance, left the security and perks of high-flying jobs in the corporate world to start their own business and put their idea to the test. They let go of the corporate mindset and instead imagined themselves as agile entrepreneurs to pursue their passion. We can prepare ourselves to jump off the cliff by asking ourselves critical questions: "Have I made all the discoveries that interest me about this world and myself? Is this it? What will I gain if I let go of what I am currently doing? Who will I become?"

Delving deeper into these questions forces us to let go of something guaranteed in favor of something potentially greater down the road. Identifying how stepping out of established territory will benefit us, curiosity acts as motivation to push through the fear of the unknown. It creates an opportunity to think about and explore something new. Research led by brain scientist Sebastian Haesler provided experimental support that experiencing a novel stimulus releases dopamine, one of the chemicals responsible for feelings of happiness.[42] In other words, putting ourselves in new situations or experiencing fresh things gets us excited. Something interesting happens. As we learn more about ourselves, we become more and more familiar with what is significant to us, what drives us, what our purpose is. "What drove me through the painful moment of learning more before I jumped into a new field was the end goal of, 'If I don't do this . . . someone needs to do that, right, and it could be me,'" Lucca explained to me.[43]

Focusing on the outcome of your project breeds a belief in yourself. In turn, this self-belief provides the energy to act on the dream. Focusing on the benefits puts the worries out of your mind. After a few weeks, you begin to have an expanded sense of possibility and the fears and doubts fade away. Will they come back? You can't know. But you can be sure that they won't be there right now.

TRY THIS

TAKE A FEW MOMENTS TO IMAGINE YOUR BEST FU-
ture self. Then ask yourself, "What will I gain if
I pursue this journey?" This exercise will work
better if you think about gains in a specific area
of your life, such as your career, relationships,
or health.

Stretch How Far You Can Go

Håkon Høydal is an award-winning investigative journalist for the Norwegian newspaper *Verdens Gang* (*VG*). Back in 2013, Høydal, with the help of another reporter, wrote a story on revenge porn. The piece exposed several people who had posted stolen nude pictures of girls. The article caught the eye of computer expert Einar Stangvik.[44] He contacted Høydal, commenting on the *VG* article and proposing how they might push the investigation further.[45]

Høydal liked what Stangvik said, and they decided to work together. They spent months tracking down the offenders of online revenge porn, including a local politician who subsequently lost his job and served a prison sentence.[46] Their investigation was a success. After publishing the article, Høydal and Stangvik combed through the websites where the pictures were posted.[47] This effort led them to other sites that seemed to be file-sharing services. They went down many rabbit holes, from which emanated other rabbit holes, many of which were terrifying for their content and extent. Stangvik went deep enough to know there was a disturbing amount of child pornography online on the so-called clearnet, that is, the publicly accessible internet.[48] In total worldwide, they found ninety-five thousand IP addresses that had downloaded child-abuse material from this handful of sites.[49]

However, both Høydal and Stangvik knew there was much more to be found on the dark web, a space for all illegal activity, including the sale of credit card numbers and drugs. The dark web can only be navigated via a specialized browser called Tor.[50] There, Høydal and Stangvik identified several child-abuse sites. Stangvik developed a complex algorithm that enabled him and Høydal to quickly sort through millions of files without their having to look at the files themselves.[51] Infiltrating the dark web, they uncovered criminal activity, and this discovery enabled them to expose the operator of the world's largest child-abuse site. This victory demonstrated to perpetrators and abusers that they were not invisible online—that they could be identified.[52]

TRY THIS

TAKE A MOMENT TO THINK ABOUT THE INTEREST THAT you want to follow. How would you go about pursuing it? Can you go any further, deeper, bigger? Think about what fears may prevent you from stretching far in your pursuit and how you can address them.

Turn Fear into Your Second Nature; Make It Part of the Curiosity Journey

Stepping outside our comfort zone is, by definition, uncomfortable. Yet it is exactly the approach we should embrace, all the time. Deliberately create opportunities to come face-to-face with your fears as much as you can. All the people I spoke with offered similar advice: Do one thing every day that scares you. And then do another, and another. The goal is to become familiar enough with facing your fears that they become a minor player in your curiosity adventures. Most of the people I talked with agree that we hold ourselves back in ways both big and small by lacking self-confidence. We lower our expectations of what we can achieve, and we tend to distance ourselves from the object of our curiosity. We must dare to step up and believe in ourselves. If we don't believe in ourselves, why should anyone else?

The act of facing your fear can be something small. Imagine you are terrified of public speaking. You could join an online class or a short in-person course. Ask people who are good at public speaking open-ended questions about how they deal with stage fright or otherwise overcome nervousness. Practice speaking in front of a friendly audience like family and friends. The majority of the people I interviewed don't sprint outside their comfort zone. They take small steps. The hardest part of getting started is that doing so can feel big and intimidating. But once you've actually begun, you are already making your fear less significant.

> *Until we can let go of old, worn-out habits, security and routines may hold us prisoners.*

Nicole Cooke grew up in Wick, South Wales, and took up cycling at an early age.[53] She was four years old when bicycles piqued her curiosity. Cooke vividly remembers how she loved being out on her bike touring the countryside and exploring new places.[54] She also remembers how her early races were a turning point. The passion turned into a dream of a cycling career. She started racing locally, and when she was twelve, Cooke joined a race in Holland and competed against the boys. She came in fifth overall.[55] Her experience in that and other races gave Cooke the confidence to believe she had a bright future in cycling. She started thinking that if she did well as a youth, she could go on to win junior world championship titles and then move on to a senior career.[56]

Combining her passion for cycling with a drive to push boundaries made her one of the most successful cyclists to ever hail from Great Britain—both in domestic competitions and on the international stage. Cooke has won Olympic and world gold medals, ten national titles, two Tour de France races, the Giro, two World Cup Series . . . and the list goes on.[57] Her greatest achievement is the 2008 double, becoming the first cyclist to win world and Olympic road race gold in the same season.[58]

Each tiny step we complete brings us closer to a sense of success and moves us forward. If we start to panic, we can look to Cooke's useful piece of advice: "Try to stay with it a little longer than you normally would before. If we stay long enough and practice often enough, it will start to become less uncomfortable," she says. "There was a British grass track championship—it's like the track but grass. I wasn't allowed to ride the senior event, but straight after the senior championship, all the same riders were going to do the same event, but it was going to just be in another format. So, I entered that event and beat the senior champion, so it wasn't in a championship race, but it was the person who was just crowned British champion." Cooke added, "After that, I wrote to British Cycling and said, 'Well, I'm obviously good enough. That knocks down one of your arguments for not putting it on,' and after that they did put it on, and they had the first-ever under-sixteen girls championships in 1998."

Focusing on what we have done, not what's left to do, gives us the confidence to do something bigger. We learn that facing our fears gives us the power to handle anything and boosts our self-esteem. We learn to trust that we will survive, regardless of what will happen. "I think there's a difference between nerves and confidence," Cooke told me. "There's the confidence of being prepared, and there are the nerves of wanting to translate your preparation into the result and the uncertainty of the tactics and things that might happen. But in terms of confidence, I always knew going into a race where I stood against my competitors."[59]

Confidence is like a muscle that grows by being stretched. As it gets stronger, we then start asking "What's next?" and the feeling is addictive. This approach may seem too simple, but it works. John Underkoffler spent fifteen years at the MIT Media

Lab, specializing in holography, animation, and visualization techniques before he was called by the famous Hollywood director Steven Spielberg to dream up human-computer interfaces for the movies.[60] Underkoffler left Boston and moved to Los Angeles. His work can be seen in the 2002 science fiction film *Minority Report*. There, Tom Cruise uses interface-enabling gloves (without a keyboard or mouse) as he whooshes through video clips of future crimes.[61]

This unique gestural interface is based on Underkoffler's early research on point-and-touch interface, called g-speak. Underkoffler's work on *Minority Report* piqued the curiosity of the business world. Several executives from *Fortune* 500 companies reached out to him, wanting to find out whether what he created for the movie was real.[62] Intrigued by various companies' interest and driven to further develop this work, Underkoffler founded Oblong Industries, a Los Angeles–based company focusing on moving the g-speak interface to the real world.

Since he jumped from academia to movies to starting his own company, I wanted to know how he became comfortable with discomfort. "I would be classified by a psychologist or a psychiatrist as an introvert, which is fine," Underkoffler told me. "As it turns out, I think a lot of entrepreneurs are, so that requires extra courage and extra energy to make professional leaps. The only reliable way that I know to overcome it is just through the pure adrenaline of excitement, the pure adrenaline of that curiosity because it allows you to step outside yourself."[63] People who have accepted their discomfort find opportunities to be "onstage" in whatever way they can and start engaging with an audience. Their acceptance of their discomfort helps them recognize fear for what it is and work through it.

GET COMFORTABLE WITH DOING THINGS WITHOUT A
plan. Jog or cycle in a new environment without
a navigation app. Go to museums, galleries, and
shops that you haven't visited before. Your mission is to start enjoying these new activities and
to let go of control.

Like daring children and youth, we can make our curiosity sur-
pass our fears. Now is the time to challenge ourselves by stepping
into the unknown. The people I talked with have had to make a
scary decision, take a big risk, or make an uncomfortable change.
You may have faced these situations, too. Do you remember what
you did? Did you leave things as they were, or did you take action?
Did you play it safe, or did you take a leap of faith?

As I am writing this book, a pandemic is changing the world.
This change is scary. It's in our nature to fear change, yet I don't
want to live life in fear; I want to maintain a healthy curiosity.
Amid the human tragedy, the global health emergency, and the
economic toll on humanity that the global pandemic has brought
to so many, there is always something positive that we can take
from even the worst situations. The pandemic didn't conquer us.
On the contrary, it helped us gain strength. We have learned to
adapt, and hopefully that tells us something about ourselves. We
aren't fixed. We are flexible. And if we embrace that kind of flex-
ibility, there are plenty of benefits to that capability. We have all
become more curious about ourselves and how we can best spend
our time, how to thrive at work, and what we can do for others.

Behind every great curiosity journey, there is someone who
took a chance and made a leap to bring their vision to life. For

some, their journeys are more personal. They are willing to trade a successful career for a life of uncertainty. For others, these leaps come in the form of ideas so groundbreaking that the new vision can reshape industries. These people want to take a chance on a mission that could well change their lives—and the world. Curiosity allows us to take more risks, ask questions unapologetically, and be unafraid of making a mistake. If we clearly recognize the fears that we face and understand how we can overcome them, those fears shrink immensely. So, let's question our fears and move forward. Choose to follow your curiosity and see where the universe takes you. The possibilities are endless.

– THE TAKEAWAYS –

- There are three fears that are likely to creep in when you embark on a curiosity journey:
  - » Fear of the unknown
  - » Impostor syndrome
  - » Fear of exposure or standing out

- There are tried-and-trusted methods for conquering your fears:
  - » Filter external noise. Mute the external world.
  - » Reframe fears as puzzles to be solved.
  - » Turn inward, and silence your inner critic.
  - » Explore who you are meant to be.
  - » Turn fear into your second nature; make it part of the curiosity process.

FOUR

Become an Expert—Fast

> *The expert at anything was once a beginner.*
>
> —HELEN HAYES (ATTRIBUTED)

MARSHALL CULPEPPER, THE SERIAL ENTREPRENEUR DISCUSSED EARLIER, says the reason he loves start-ups is that you "spend a lot of time building a path that is not an easy one. You've got to work through the ambiguity, and it takes creativity, and it takes resourcefulness. And honestly, sometimes, it takes a lot of wrong turns to get there."[1] As described earlier, Culpepper was so filled with curiosity about a start-up's attempts to use the open-source platform Arduinos in space that he wound up working for the start-up and ultimately founded his own venture, KubOS.[2] Culpepper had to become an expert quickly, but he faced a significant challenge. He had neither the formal qualifications nor the relevant experience in astronomy. Undeterred by his own naivety and seduced by the business opportunity, Culpepper immersed himself in the science of astronomy. Searching online for insights proved very useful, but what he found particularly useful was Coursera's online course on astronomy and aerospace engineering.[3] Culpepper's goal was simply getting a framework to build on for the knowledge he would need for his new position.

Like Culpepper, many people who work nine to five decide to teach themselves new skills, launch a business, or explore any new area of interest. Eager to pursue their curiosity journeys, the lack of relevant formal qualification or experience does not deter them. Even those who have some background in a subject soon realize that they must push the boundaries of their knowledge further. The knowledge behind their area of expertise may be so cutting-edge that even a recent university education may be insufficient. Curious individuals must learn to absorb new knowledge and skills in a short amount of time. Fortunately, there are tactics and tools that can get you up to speed with a new domain.

> *Give yourself permission*
> *to focus on your studies.*
> *The latest Instagram post will*
> *be there when you are finished.*

BECOME YOUR OWN HEAD OF SCHOOL

When you are seized with a passion to learn as much as you can about the subject that stirs your curiosity, you can create your own learning environment, set your learning goals, and plan your own lessons. Begin with focus: Determine as precisely as you can what you want to learn, and then decide which structure will best help you achieve that goal. Do you need a quiet space for reading, writing, and reflection, or perhaps a workshop equipped with appropriate tools? Be aware that when you first delve into a subject, the information available can seem overwhelming. You need not be daunted, but you do need to make informed judgments about not only the quality and reliability of the information you are discovering but also about its relevance to your learning goal. As head of school, you must tackle several tasks:

- Establish your framework.
- Create your own curriculum.
- Build your own community.
- Become a conversation connoisseur.
- Piece the puzzle together.

Establish Your Framework

Be specific about your learning goals. What do you want to know? Develop a timetable for the subjects that you want to study. As a measure of your own time, keep in mind that typical college courses run roughly three hours per week for fourteen weeks, or one semester. In addition, there is time spent working on class assignments, up to another five hours a week. Try to dedicate a similar number of hours per week to learning (around eight). There are creative ways to find the time. Turn your daily commute into a class: on public transportation, tune out the noise and use the time to read. If you are driving, listen to podcasts or audiobooks. Focus your energy on your new curiosity project.

Create your schedule and stick to it, and do not be discouraged if you find the routine difficult at first. Concentration is a mental muscle, and if it has atrophied, we have to train it back into shape. Concentrate for short periods on a book or an article that you read online. Focus on what you are doing right now, not on what you did yesterday or what you will be doing tomorrow. Remember to also plan for breaks. If you find yourself needing more time, add more semesters. Two simple ground rules will help you get more out of your self-made classes: stick to a routine, and self-impose solitude.

Stick to a Routine

When Vern Brownell took over as CEO of D-Wave, the previously mentioned quantum computing company, in 2009, he knew he had to supplement his deep knowledge of classical computing with knowledge of the new field of quantum computing. So, he turned to the experts for a crash course: he organized tutorials that got him up to speed with the field.[4] "I did an hour tutorial a day with D-Wave scientists," Brownell recalls. "They helped me learn at my own pace until I was up to speed on the technology."[5] When you create your own learning curriculum, routines and self-discipline are a must. Creating a structure for yourself can give you a sense of order to make the most of the present.

Self-Impose Solitude

Because our lives are filled with distractions, it is no accident that people bent on satisfying their curiosity itch will self-impose the discipline of solitude. Find a quiet, private space at home or in your office that you can claim as your study space. If such a space is simply not available, seek out a quiet space in your local library. If all else fails, use noise-canceling headphones to avoid distractions. Put your other devices away. Impose a social media ban during your study time. If you have to use a laptop, tablet, or phone to read something, then close all your social media apps and turn off all notifications. Give yourself permission to focus on your studies. The latest Instagram post will be there when you are finished.

Olly Olsen cofounded the Office Group in 2003. Since then, the company has expanded exponentially by creating more than fifty beautifully designed flexible workspaces across the United Kingdom and Germany; these spaces are now the offices of more than twenty thousand members.[6] When asked about tackling a new curiosity project, Olsen answered thoughtfully, stressing the importance of solitude: "It could be a walk in the park. It could be a journey. It could be any way to distance yourself."[7] Olsen does not minimize the difficulty of achieving solitude, noting that there are very few places where you cannot connect to the broader world through the internet or truly retreat from the company of others. Still, he says, "It's when I disconnect myself from all technology and disconnect myself from all other human interaction—these are the times when my curiosity is most productive."

Create Your Own Curriculum

You have set aside the time you need to study, and you have claimed a distraction-free place for your work. Now comes the hard part— but it is also the fun part: gathering the resources you will require to master the material you need to know to fulfill your curiosity.

Where do you begin? Most of the time, this is a trial-and-error process. To get up-to-date quickly and build useful and relevant knowledge in a new domain, live by two basic rules: Filter useful information from the noise, and do not believe everything you read. In other words, evaluate material as you discover it. Is it from an authoritative source? Is it up-to-date? Has it been reviewed by experts in the field? The curious people interviewed for this book have a range of ways to determine whether a source was worth pursuing. They realize that there is much good advice out there, but they do not have to follow all of it. They develop ways to isolate the noise from important knowledge by differentiating between what they *must* learn and what would be nice to learn. Again, the lesson here is focus. For example, Hazel Forsyth, senior curator of the medieval and post-medieval collections at the Museum of London, says that setting a limit on reading time helps her focus on the materials she needs to master.[8]

Luckily for us, the experts I interviewed offer advice on navigating new areas of interest and deepen our understanding. It looks like a curriculum with three intensive courses: CUR101, the art of searching online; CUR102, immersing yourself in your new domain; and CUR103, practicing disciplined serendipity.

CUR101: The Art of Searching Online:
Do Not Start from a Blank Page

The internet has excellent resources, but what you need is often more than one click away. So before you resort to brute force and run every conceivable search you can think of using your emerging parameters, set some time constraints and focus. Start by gaining a broader understanding of the new area by reviewing other people's work online. Knowledge that has already been collected and disseminated by others has two key benefits. First, you understand the state of the field by looking at what others are doing, and you can build on that to make further improvements. Ask two questions: What is really new? What is really interesting? After a while, you will develop your own knowledge and understanding that will form the foundation of your curiosity project and can help you stretch the boundaries further. Second, knowing what is already out there will make you sound more credible when you conduct your own primary research to discover stuff yourself (e.g., by talking directly to experts).

By becoming purposefully curious, we can more easily soak up expertise from a wide range of internet sources: articles, academic studies, reports, blog posts, online tutorials, and courses, which are accessible to all of us. Favored sources are categorized by the material they contain. For example, you can consult social media (e.g., Facebook and Twitter) and trusted news publications (e.g., the *New York Times*, *Financial Times*, the *Economist*, and *Scientific American*). You can also seek out specialized publications and open-access repositories (like arXiv, a free distribution service and archive of scientific papers in mathematics, physics, astronomy, electrical engineering, computer science, quantitative biology, statistics, mathematical finance, and economics).[9] You can tap educational platforms like Coursera, online communities (e.g., Kaggle for data scientists and machine learning practitioners), or other online courses offered by universities globally. You can also use other tools such as news aggregators (e.g., Google Alerts) and applications (e.g., Feedly) that prioritize articles from the feeds you have selected.

When we practice purposeful curiosity, we can make our online searches more dynamic by enriching them with podcasts and documentaries on topics and content that genuinely inspire us. We can enjoy a forensic search of videos on YouTube, Vimeo, or TED and listen to podcasts on history, technology, science, or even detective stories—whatever strikes our fancy and adds to the journey we're on.

Use these guidelines as you begin your research:

1. Find the leading blogs, podcasts, documentaries, and other publications in your new field.
2. Identify the top minds (e.g., academics, scientists, entrepreneurs, mavericks) in this field. Who else is emerging?
3. Look up the leading organizations and businesses (e.g., start-ups) in this area.

CUR102: Immersing Yourself in Your New Domain: Dig Deeper

Curious people do not rely exclusively on digitized resources. They balance screen time with field trips; they flesh out their self-created curriculum by searching through archives, learning from specialists, and going "off-piste."

VISIT AN ARCHIVE

A couple of times per week, I go on inspiration-gathering walks. I visit museums, art galleries, and other places where inspiration might strike. In one of these walks, I came across a special exhibition at the Victoria and Albert Museum's Gilbert Galleries. Jacques Schuhmacher and his colleague Alice Minter curated the pioneering exhibition *Concealed Histories: Uncovering the Story of Nazi Looting*, providing invaluable insights into the provenance of certain museum objects and the history of their ownership.[10] I spent an afternoon going through the exhibited objects and reading about their troubling history through a detailed exhibition guide that the curators had created.

Intrigued by this interesting collection and reading a section titled "How Do You Research Something That Doesn't Want to Be Found?" from the exhibition guide, I reached out to Schuhmacher to learn more about how he conducts provenance research in such a sensitive matter. "Nothing beats actual archival research," he told me. "It depends on the subject that you are investigating, but you have to think where the thing that you want to find out about may have left a trace, a document, somewhere else. That might not be immediately obvious. For example, you should not just look in the files of Nazi institutions just because the Nazis were the ones who took Jewish property. You also have to look at the files of German art dealers who may have sold Jewish properties on behalf of German Jews who wanted to be able to leave the country. You would want to look at maybe what the records that were created by families or records that were created in the countries where they went to, where they then told people about what the experience was in Germany at that time. You might want to look at memoirs or family correspondence and photographs that might depict these objects. You might want to look at newspapers or journals and magazines to see if there's an object shown in those sources."[11]

Schuhmacher worked his way backward in time until it became clear who owned the object before and during the Nazi period. He also spent considerable time going through scholarly literature or the catalogs published by auction houses or proud collectors for traces of the objects in question. This imaginative engagement with past texts, images, and objects offers invaluable insights that more conventional digital searches might struggle to find.

LEARN FROM SPECIALISTS

Vern Brownell suggests asking the experts for recommendations.[12] If you are using a library, ask for assistance in identifying a reliable and useful source of information. Librarians are trained in doing this work—so take advantage of their expertise. Or go straight to an authority. Check out college and university websites. Look at course descriptions relevant to your subject matter, and then see if the professor has made the class syllabus available online. This course outline and reading list will give you a great place to start when you are looking for reliable research materials. Lionel Barber, award-winning English journalist and editor of the *Financial Times* from 2005 to 2020, suggests doing a quick scan of a book or an article to see if it meets your needs.[13]

A tough critic, Barber stresses how important it is to make judgments quickly when you are under time constraints. "Make your mind up fairly quickly about whether [a source] is worth reading," Barber says. "I give somebody usually five paragraphs to see if I can detect a thesis that will be important to my work."[14] If he does not think he will find what he is looking for, Barber sets the text aside and moves on. Unsurprisingly, purposefully curious people don't simply accept what they hear or read at face value; instead, they focus on finding out more about it. They are very careful about what is on the internet. They are not passive readers but are active doubters. They check the quality of what they are absorbing.

Indulge in a visit to a bookstore; unearth writings from specialists in the new domain. Search the aisles long enough to discover something intriguing. Don't hesitate to seek out books that are quick and easy to read. Jólan van der Wiel, the award-winning Dutch experimental designer introduced earlier in the book, explained that he often heads to the children's and young adult sections of the library when learning about an unfamiliar topic. "I like space magazines and books. And in many cases when I am trying to understand a topic, I go to the children's department because I can find books that explain a new (to me) topic clearly and simply. That's a quick way of learning about a topic."[15]

> *Imaginative engagement with past texts, images, and objects offers invaluable insights that more conventional digital searches might struggle to find.*

Go Off-Piste

Immersing ourselves in our own or another culture can also be an eye-opening learning experience about a new field. I call this tactic *going off-piste*, using the same phrase that skiers use for venturing onto a trackless, still-unblazed trail. Curious people often dive into food, the design scene, hubs, institutions, and historical landmarks for insight into how people live and how things work. Artist Gavin Turk explained to me how, on one of his cultural trips to Moscow, he spent a day at the house of a person he had just met. "I met this person randomly," Turk said, "who invited me to his house, a very small apartment full of books. A friend of his came around and sang Russian folk songs and told stories. People turn their flats into galleries and take turns in going to visit the rooms where people were having exhibitions."[16] He experienced the culture with all his senses. Chatting with people, hearing their stories, and understanding their lives were memorable and informative experiences.[17]

CUR103: Practicing Disciplined Serendipity

The curious people I talked to make room for *disciplined serendipity* in their learning. This habit is a bit like visiting a library or a bookshop and browsing bookshelves that are unrelated to what you came in to study. On these random shelves, you nevertheless find books that are broadly relevant to your subject or—more importantly—inspiring. Learning how to practice disciplined serendipity should be an essential part of your curriculum.

First, if we want to be more curious, we need to have more things to connect. The best way to build a rich database that will help us later solve problems is to honor our ephemeral curiosities, as John Underkoffler told me during our conversation about the value of serendipity. "That is the moment, that is the fun," he said. "I love hearing about a scientist or an artist that I'd never heard about before. Now I have a new thing to learn about. It rekindles the curiosity candle; the flame starts again."[18] You can create such moments for yourself by drawing up a list of books, papers, conference sessions, and videos that seem to have little immediate value. Spend time going through them. I guarantee you that following these serendipitous paths will pay off. As with other research, though, put a time limit on your foray into the serendipitous. Keep track of your disciplined serendipity time. Limit your serendipity time to 15–20 percent of your total research time. Recognize that if you go beyond this limit, you may be sabotaging the rest of your research.

Curious people also understand that we ultimately tend to experience life in an echo chamber. Not surprisingly, then, these people feed themselves different things. They create the anti-reading list, which includes publications, blogs, podcasts, and videos that offer the opposite perspective. They also connect with proponents of other perspectives and try to understand what information has led these other people to conclusions contrary to their own.

Curious people sometimes realize that what they are about to embark on has not been done before. Martin Frost, the aforementioned cofounder of CMR Surgical, the leading company behind surgical robotic systems, took the company from start-up to unicorn status (i.e., a valuation of $1 billion or more) in less than six years. Frost believes that even when there is no existing knowledge on the subject that has excited your curiosity, you may be able to learn from other extraordinary journeys: "Of course, I'm interested and read all of the research on medical devices," Frost says. "What fascinates me are the journeys that other entrepreneurs have done that have moved the dial in a different industry and then trying to learn and apply those lessons in this market. I can't go and read the book on how to go and build a big medical device company here in the UK, because that book hasn't been written. We can't follow the journey another company has made in this space in this country. So that means you end up trying to learn lessons from journeys that other people have been on and then applying those lessons to this particular journey."[19]

Showing curiosity, asking questions, and discovering something interesting about another person gets people to share more and prompts them to ask questions.

Build Your Own Community

Stretching the boundaries of your chosen domain is also about developing a diverse, strong, and growing network and building your own community of mentors and advisers. Curious people soak up expertise from a wide range of sources and diligently acknowledge people who have helped them along the way. At the beginning of your curiosity journey, devote time to your support system. You must initially build your community on your own, but as it slowly grows, your network will evolve organically.

Become a Conversation Connoisseur

Curiosity means reaching out. Talking to strangers is generally more challenging than talking to people we know, but reaching out like this is ultimately more rewarding. It helps us grow our network, raises our profile, and expands our empathy. We become better able to see inside the head of the other person—the life, experience, and worldview, all of which are different from our own.[20] We often think that we would not enjoy interacting with people we do not know, but research by psychology professors Erica Boothby and Gus Cooney of the University of Pennsylvania, Gillian Sandstrom of the University of Sussex, and Margaret Clark of Yale University suggests the opposite: We will like it more than we think.[21] Actually, interactions with a stranger—not a friend or a loved one—can contribute meaningfully to our happiness.[22] Why? It makes us feel connected.

Whom do you need to talk to? Think about who has already had some degree of success in the new domain, and learn how they did it. Modeling part of their approach means that you can gain an advantage without having to reinvent anything. To build their own community, curious people reach out to experts, find fellow curious people, and focus on outreach.

<hr>

TRY THIS

BE BRAVE. SET YOURSELF THE CHALLENGE OF HAVING a conversation with one stranger every week (e.g., a dog owner, gym classmate, coffee barista).

<hr>

Reach Out to Experts

Polar explorer Ben Saunders told me how reaching out to people who have achieved similar goals gave him invaluable insights and knowledge that informed his challenging expeditions.[23]

Building up a network of experts who have different and, sometimes, niche knowledge around the world is critical, yet it takes time. Says Saunders, "I have found lots of specialists in very small niches, whether it was things like satellite tracking, GPS, [and subjects from] nutrition to physical training to even the clothing. I have a guy based in Wales who hand-makes expedition clothing, tiny little business. There's somebody in Norway that makes my sledges; they're handmade from Kevlar and carbon fiber."[24]

Read books, case studies, and academic research or reports to familiarize yourself with the new domain *before* contacting people who know about the subject. Get up-to-date about the latest developments and other relevant information so that you don't waste the expert's time. You may feel intimidated by reaching out to experts in your new field, and, yes, doing so can be difficult at first. Fortunately, there are steps you can follow to reduce your anxiety and increase your chances for success in scoring a meeting. The most important things to keep in mind are to be well prepared, polite, and respectful.

Begin with prep—then prep some more. Once you identify the people you want to talk to and set up a meeting, make sure you overprepare. Before you meet, read as much as you can about them. Find their bios online (through company or personal websites or LinkedIn), read news articles about them, go through any interviews they have given, and watch their videos. Familiarize yourself with the person and their journey. Identifying commonalities or aspects worth commenting on in your meeting will help you build rapport and keep them at ease at the beginning.

Then, identify questions or topics that you would like to explore in your conversation. Write them down. Having a guide for your conversation will help you feel more relaxed and confident and will show that you respect the expert's time. In addition, a written list will ensure that you do not forget an important issue that you may not get a second chance to ask about.

Request your meeting by sending a personal invitation letter or email that is clear about your intentions. Include any relevant information that lends credibility to you and your project, for example, the name of the person who introduced you to them or the names of others you have interviewed to illustrate who you are and why it would be great to meet. See the sample text in the box.

═══ INVITATION LETTER OR EMAIL ═══

_____ (add the full address of the person you are reaching out to)

_____ (date)

Dear _____ (name),

This is _____ (your name), _____ (your title and company or organization affiliation).

For the past _____weeks/months/years (how long you have been working on this), I have been interviewing world-renowned thought leaders on _____ (the focus of your project) for a _____ (the deliverable/contribution: a book, product, report, TED talk, etc.). _____ (write a couple of sentences about your fascination with the topic. For instance: Why do you feel this domain is important? Why now?). _____ (the gap that you aim to fill) is largely unknown.

I am fascinated by your profile as an accomplished _____ (write about what makes them special). You _____ (write about a particular incident that intrigued you and the reason why you are reaching out to them). Since _____ (write something about their superpower) propels your work into new grounds, I felt that you would be one of the most enlightening people in your field that I could interview.

So far, I've interviewed high performers across the globe from diverse fields, including _____ (mention the industries) (e.g., _____ add some representative names). I would welcome the opportunity to schedule an informational interview with you to understand more _____ (the main area that you would like to discuss).

I know that you must be quite busy, so I assure you I will be brief. Who is the best person to contact in your organization to inquire about a convenient time for scheduling a meeting or phone call? You can also reach me at _____ (your mobile number) or at _____ (your email address).

Thank you very much for considering this request.

Sincerely,

_____ (your name)

GET THE BEST OUT OF THE CONVERSATION

Curious people who have found a passion in their lives can be warm, courteous, and generous with their time, knowledge, and contacts. In my experience, when you reach out to someone whose curiosity has helped catapult them to the top of their field, they will ask *you* questions because they are naturally curious. They want to learn about you, too. Psychology professors Todd Kashdan and Patrick McKnight of George Mason University, Frank Fincham of Florida State University, and Paul Rose of Southern Illinois University Edwardsville asked participants in a study to either have an intimate conversation or make small talk with strangers. After engaging in these types of conversations, the participants who were more curious felt closer to their conversational partner in both situations, while less curious people did not.[25] Showing curiosity, asking questions, and discovering something interesting about another person gets people to share more and prompts them to ask questions. Their study shows that a spirit of give-and-take fosters intimacy.

But what actually leads to a great conversation with an expert whom you are trying to engage in a network? There are three ground rules.

First, aim to build rapport, but do not try to sell yourself. If the person has agreed to have a conversation with you, then you have already accomplished some measure of rapport. Remind them that you are not an expert and that you are starting your journey. Listen for things you have in common, and use those commonalities to build a gradual rapport. Set a friendly tone. This is not a time for small talk, but at the beginning, you do want to make the conversation relaxed.

Second, come across as an interested inquirer, not an interrogator. As an academic who does research by interviewing and observing people in their workplaces, I cannot overstress the importance of showing real interest—it is almost like a process of seduction. A good conversation is not about interrogating someone but is about listening carefully to what they have to say. At one point, people will eventually let you in; they will open their doors and hand down their knowledge.

Nigel Toon, the cofounder and CEO of Graphcore, an AI computer maker, is responsible for revolutionizing the global chip-making industry and taking the company from its humble beginnings in 2012 to unicorn status in 2018. In this amazing journey, Toon talked with diverse experts, including scientists, engineers, and investors. "It's also a psychological thing, when you work with other people," Toon says, "if you make them feel good, make them feel they're the expert, make them feel they're the teacher. They feel good, and they'll share more information with you in a very open manner. And if you listen well, [if] you listen actively and encourage them, you can actually encourage them to probably explain a lot more to you, and to tell you a lot more, than they might normally."[26]

People love talking about themselves, and asking a few well-chosen questions has the psychological effect of making you seem interesting, too, so the dialogue gets going. Another study by psychology professors Todd Kashdan of George Mason University and John Roberts of the University at Buffalo found that people were rated as warmer and more attractive if they showed real curiosity in an exchange.[27] Demonstrating curiosity about someone is a great way to build closeness with them. It makes sense that someone who is curious is likely to be better at connecting with strangers.

Third, ask open-ended questions to get your responder to go deeper. Closed-ended questions, or questions with yes-or-no answers, neither encourage conversation nor spark new ideas in your respondent. Think like a journalist, which in a sense you are, and ask the questions a reporter would ask: *What, who, why, when, where,* and *how* questions push the respondent to think and reflect on their own terms and without a barrier. Allow your respondent time to think about questions you ask; a quiet moment of reflection will yield a thoughtful answer. For instance, several of the entrepreneurs interviewed for this book started their curiosity journeys by meeting a range of experts or potential users of their products and trying to understand their working patterns, needs, and wants by asking open-ended questions such as these: How did you start this? How do you do your work? What's involved? What are the challenges? Asking follow-up questions that probe for deeper understanding will make your respondent excited and help you to delve deeper.

Beware of questions that contain hidden assumptions. Instead of "What made you decide to become a space explorer?" it is better to ask, "How did it happen that you became a space explorer?" Avoid jumping to conclusions. Keep your curiosity mindset and always ask why. Our curiosity journeys will greatly benefit from asking open-ended questions since we are looking for answers, explanations, stories, and insights that are truly unknown to us. Start taking copious notes, or get the person's permission to record conversations up front.

Finally, do not feel threatened by the technical language or details that initially sound like a foreign language. If you are really at a loss to understand something that has just been said, say so. Use the wrap-up time during the conversation to ask a few debrief questions to help you sift through some of the most important insights or areas that require further clarification or to solicit overarching thoughts, impressions, or conclusions. With time and more research, everything will start becoming clearer. At the end of the conversation, thank your experts right away.

THANK AND RECIPROCATE

Write a thank-you note or email. Personalize your message, and let your interviewees know what you have learned from them, how they contributed, and how they made a difference in your journey. Ideally, you want to form an ongoing relationship. This is your chance to offer something of value, to reciprocate the favor. Stay in touch, and try to give back. Take a look at the sample thank-you letter provided.

SAMPLE THANK-YOU LETTER

Dear _____ (name of the person),

Thank you for sharing your invaluable insights with me on _____ (date of the conversation). I appreciate the time you took to talk with me. If I can reciprocate in any way, please let me know. You shared many valuable points, such as _____ (something insightful that they shared), _____ (something awesome that you observed), _____ (something that changed how you see this domain), and I'm grateful for them.

Have a great week, and thank you again!

FIND THE FELLOW CURIOUS

Learning is no fun in a vacuum. Find other curious people with whom you can discuss your journeys and ideas. These associations need not be with recognized experts to be inspiring. Zowie Broach, the head of fashion at London's Royal College of Art and renowned for her avant-garde, fashion-meets-art design label,

Boudicca, emphasizes the value of being surrounded by other curious people. "I've trained under great people who taught patterns of curiosity," Broach says, "and who taught me that we are drawn to other curious people to watch their patterns and learn under their patterns."[28]

The question, then, is how do you find other curious people? Bompas & Parr, an avant-garde experiential food and event company based in London, is globally recognized as the leader in multisensory experience design. It pushes the boundaries and helps people learn something along the way. Cofounder Sam Bompas makes it a point to attend talks of people embarking on their own curiosity journeys: "Often the talks I enjoy seeing the most are not necessarily by the accomplished speaker who knows lots and has presented in all sorts of scenarios," he told me. "It is when the person is often very nervous, it is a new thing, but they really care about what they are doing. I am always trying to get into new things, like niche things."[29]

Look for people whose curiosity is genuine. Jon Wiley, introduced in an earlier chapter, was formerly a senior director at Google responsible for innovations like Google Cardboard, Google Expeditions, and the Daydream VR platform and Daydream View VR headset (among many others). Wiley has made it a priority to attend invitation-only ORD Camp, which he describes as a mix of scientists, artists, creators, and technologists—every kind of curious person. He attends conferences and "unconferences" (where anything goes in terms of presentations and topics) to immerse himself in environments where there are curious people from many domains adjacent to, or far-flung from, his own.[30] Wiley explains that connecting with them is critical since they may be asking similar questions or may have already walked the path he is interested in walking.[31]

If you are really at a loss to understand something that has just been said, say so.

GET YOUR MESSAGE OUT

While working on his master's degree in fashion at the Royal College of Art in 2017, Louis Alderson-Bythell entered the RCA's 2017 Biodesign Challenge.[32] Alderson-Bythell had always been fascinated by the production processes in fashion and how to improve them for the benefit of society.[33] This time, though, Alderson-Bythell's curiosity was triggered not by an object in fashion but by a process in another, radically unrelated and new domain: agriculture, more precisely, pollination. Alderson-Bythell immersed himself in that domain. His preliminary research unearthed some disturbing insights. Bees, the largest group of pollinators, have been declining significantly because of industrial agriculture, pesticides, and a changing climate.[34] Alderson-Bythell and his colleagues brainstormed ways to slow this decline and came up with an idea that satisfied them. The idea was to encourage flies (which account for 30 percent of global pollination) to be more efficient pollinators in scenarios where bee pollination would no longer be viable.[35] Their new and exciting agricultural technology, which Alderson-Bythell and his group pitched to a panel from academia and industry, manages fly behavior (via the release of natural volatiles and carefully curated chemicals into a field) to aid the pollination process.[36] Alderson-Bythell and his team won the first prize and some seed funding from the university to turn this project into a company, Olombria.[37]

Curious people follow a robust method to build their outreach and get their message out. They create platforms with multilateral flows of information and, in doing so, disseminate knowledge about their curiosity projects or journeys to as many interested parties as possible. Having a genuine give-and-take dynamic builds trust, which in turn plants the seeds for ongoing alliances that may lead to more complex knowledge exchanges.

Alderson-Bythell discussed how this exchange works in practice. "We spoke to a lot of people, and we still do have a massive network of people that we can speak to really regularly. When you speak to other people, they often present you with ideas that you would never have considered. We've had papers shared with us, we've had books sent to us in the post, we've sent books out to people, shared research papers with researchers who hadn't seen the material we'd seen. It's crazy how sharing happens. Even hoverfly researchers working in India had research material that was interesting for us."[38]

Curious people use their newfound knowledge and persuasive power to educate and share information around their curiosity projects. As a museum senior curator, Hazel Forsyth spent years studying objects, letters, stock lists, and rent books to uncover Elizabethan and early Stuart jewelers' trade and, by extension, life and fashion in London society of the era.[39] Her painstaking research turned into a book, *The Cheapside Hoard: London's Lost Jewels*, and an accompanying exhibition.[40] Forsyth's next curiosity project focused on exploring other intriguing questions: What happened to London after the Great Fire in 1666? What impact did the fire have on individual lives? And how did Londoners—particularly women—survive? She spent a lot of time researching livery company records, letters, diaries, and legal and municipal documents and inventories, trying to gain a picture of domestic and corporate loss.[41]

In her fascinating book *Butcher, Baker, Candlestick Maker*, Forsyth traces how citizens, institutions, and traders, from apothecaries and bakers to upholsterers and watchmakers, rebuilt lives and London's former prosperity.[42] Digging deeper into these fascinating areas and uncovering evidence to build engaging, coherent, and novel insights, Forsyth emphasizes the value in sharing the fruits of her research with any interested parties. "It is trying to find ways to engage people and to make contacts. Sometimes after giving a lecture people come up to you afterward and they say, 'I know so-and-so,' or they hand you a business card, and then it's up to you to decide whether you want to develop that contact. Sometimes people out of the blue write in and say, 'Have you any information?' and then you wonder if they might know somebody whom you might talk to. I've been very grateful for friends and acquaintances recommending people that I should talk to and linking me up with people whom I perhaps otherwise wouldn't have known about."[43]

Besides starting an outreach network, curious people focus on enlarging it. As you get your message out, you build relationships with people and organizations, and more information is shared. You spend time researching, identifying, and reaching out to different individuals with different kinds of knowledge. You bring people together and participate in or lead conversations around your new area of interest and its future. Regular workshops or seminar series can be great ways to invite experts to highlight the opportunities and challenges in their chosen domain and to help other participants in the network. Indeed, curious people are aware that they cannot know everything and must find ways of enabling other people to contribute to and engage with their journeys. Network heterogeneity enables breadth and depth of knowledge, and ambitious projects act as magnets for diverse networks.

Outreach networks can do wonders over time. For example, Schuhmacher explained how by putting the objects on display at the Victoria and Albert Museum, the curators hope that a visitor might recognize an object and share further ideas about its provenance.[44] Curious people know that creating and maintaining relationships is an investment that does not typically yield its full harvest in the short run but can be rewarding in the long term. So, they keep in contact with many people who have an interest in their domain. They maintain reciprocal relationships, and, more often than not, the networks cultivate new connections.

Piece Together the Puzzle

What makes curious people become experts fast is their ability to master the best of what other people have already figured out—to build their curiosity projects on preexisting knowledge. They are experts in creating value by assembling collections of knowledge. Joseph Henrich, professor of human evolutionary biology at Harvard University, made a case in his book *The Secret of Our Success* that humans are successful as a species because they do not need to learn everything from scratch; they can build upon the body of knowledge our culture has accumulated.[45]

Before curious explorers visit their destinations, they pull together all the information that they can, including hot tips and recommendations from the internet or locals. "If I'm trying to do something new," Greek-Canadian adventurer Kourounis enthusiastically told me, "I will grab every single photo on the internet that I can find, from every single angle, that anyone has uploaded, that's even remotely similar, and I will just amass all of that, and I'll be able to construct a three-dimensional model in my mind of what's going on, so that when I arrive on-site, I have fewer surprises."[46]

There are many ways to piece together all the information that you have gathered. Let's look at three of them.

Read Actively

Block out time in your schedule, and commit to methodically checking off the resources that you have collected. Your sources could be printed or digital, fiction or nonfiction, magazines, news-papers, annual reports, blogs. Keep track of insights you amass along the way. When you start a new curiosity project, you must become not only a voracious reader but also an active one. When you are an active reader, journalist Lionel Barber says, you are "looking for things that are new, surprising—the kind of things that force you to ask, 'What's that about?' You really have to focus and concentrate to put yourself in an active moment."[47]

Look for Interesting Insights

Review your notes, and start looking for patterns. Make sense of all the articles, meeting notes, academic research, white papers, and industry reports. Your mission is to generate some interesting insights, says Nigel Toon: "You need to go through phases of acquiring the information, and then you need phases of contemplation to work out, 'OK, so how do I process that, and what's important, and what did I really learn from that?'"[48] Synthesize what is happening around your domain. Turn this into a systematic process and stick to it! Use Post-it notes or a whiteboard to organize common themes from your research. What are you finding? Any interesting insights or patterns? Going through what you collected will generate new ideas, which also need further researching. Make a note of them, and add more questions to be used in future conversations with experts or other like-minded people.

Purposefully curious people can easily shift between subjects and synthesize the material for their own purposes. Saunders, the polar explorer, preparing for the Scott Expedition in 2013–2014 (the same Antarctic expedition that killed Captain Robert Falcon Scott and his men over a distance of almost sixteen hundred miles), sought to learn not only from more than a hundred years' worth of expeditions but also from disparate sources, including ultra-endurance athletes and doctors treating patients who lose weight during chemotherapy.[49] By hopping borders normally walled off to experts and grasping lessons from one area to inform another while seeking links between them, Saunders could better deal with uncertainty and ultimately rewrite history by completing the ill-fated journey of Captain Scott's iconic expedition.

> *Curious people know that creating and maintaining relationships is an investment that does not typically yield its full harvest in the short run but can be rewarding in the long term.*

Spot What Others Have Missed

To create valuable and actionable knowledge, curious people also focus on spotting what others have missed. Scrutinize the minutiae. Your potential returns are higher if you spend time looking at the smallest details that others may have missed or are not telling. Novelist Michael Robotham says that going through newspapers and magazines can plant the seed for a new book. "Probably the best example I can give is [my] book that won the UK Gold Dagger in 2015, *Life or Death*," he said. "It began on March 20, 1985. I read a two-paragraph story in a newspaper about a man who served two life sentences. He'd been jailed for two murders and served over thirty years in prison, and he escaped the day before he was due to be released. And I just thought, 'Why does a man escape from prison the day before he's due to be released?' I carried that cutting around with me for twenty years thinking, 'There's a novel in this somewhere, but I have to think of a reason why someone would do it. Why someone would escape the day beforehand.' Now I had a vague idea why he might escape from jail, but I had no idea what was going to come next."[50]

Robotham became curious to know what may have gone through the escapee's mind. He also goes through the obituaries sections and collects stories of scientists, soldiers, or adventurers—unsung heroes, people who are not household names yet who have had the most astonishing lives.[51] These tiny and constant research projects enrich the book ideas that he wants to start or move his current projects forward.

To hone their new knowledge, curious people recognize that learning is ongoing. Your new life may require a new set of skills—and you have to be honest enough with yourself about what you are and are not good at. Set aside several weeks, months, or years (or even your entire lifetime) to arm yourself with up-to-date expertise to master the new area, to build up your accumulated and compounded knowledge. In D-Wave Systems, the founders spent five years surveying the scientific literature and doing pointed collaborations with several universities around the world before they decided to build a particular kind of quantum computer and launch their business.[52] It is, therefore, not unheard-of to take considerable time and sustained effort to build significant understanding around a new field.

– THE TAKEAWAYS –

- The best way to learn about your new passion is to teach yourself. Go back to school by creating your own curriculum. Develop a timetable, stick to that routine, and engage in self-imposed solitude.
- Develop focus by setting aside time each day to read or work on your project.

- Select what is important by filtering the noise and questioning everything you read. Pursue three core curriculum subjects: the art of searching online, immersing yourself in your new domain, and practicing disciplined serendipity.
- Build your own community. Reach out to experts, find fellow curious, and crowdsource wisdom by developing an outreach program. Don't be afraid to ask questions.
- Ace your informational interviews by following the three-act conversation plan: prepare, get the best out of the conversation, and thank and reciprocate.
- Piece together the puzzle by actively reading, looking for interesting insights, and spotting what others have missed.
- Curious people get themselves up-to-date quickly to make progress with their curiosity project, yet they also recognize that learning is an ongoing process. It takes considerable time and sustained effort to build significant understanding.
- Guard against information overload by honing your ability to recognize useful sources.

FIVE

Ask, "Who's with Me?"

> *Alone, we can do so little; together, we can
> do so much.*
>
> —HELEN KELLER

IN 2016, THIEME HENNIS WAS FINISHING HIS PHD IN COMPLEX SYStems design at the Delft University of Technology in the Netherlands when he became intrigued by cross-disciplinary conversations in science, ecology, and technology.[1] Long driven by a desire to create a better world for the next generation, Hennis became instrumental in developing programs for Border Sessions. This annual tech cultural festival in The Hague, Netherlands, offers a variety of events and workshops aimed at how new technologies can be used for positive social and environmental change. The multiday event brings together a variety of people, including writers, researchers, artists, activists, engineers, and designers, to present and discuss their latest work on cutting-edge developments in technology (e.g., drones, robotics, biohacking).[2] When the European Space Agency (ESA) presented at one of the event's workshops, the session caught Hennis's attention.[3] Included in the seminar was a discussion of how plants perform in different environments, as plants are a core element of the life-support system.

MELiSSA (Micro-Ecological Life Support System Alternative) was founded by ESA in 1989 to create a life-support system for space, to minimize the cargo needed for human missions to the moon and Mars.[4] Understanding plants and being able to control their growth was critical to MELiSSA's success. In the seminar, it became apparent that citizens could be empowered to assist ME-LiSSA's mission to characterize a large number of plant species and cultivars and evaluate crop data for space-farming potential.[5] Connecting people to the thrilling challenge of building self-sustainable ecosystems in space and educating them about critical technologies required to keep our planet livable seemed like an exciting possibility and got Hennis's attention. In response, he launched AstroPlant, an open-source project to create small-scale artificial ecosystems for space. As the project's "mission commander," Hennis built an educational platform for innovation and research for controlled-environment agriculture and beyond.[6] Right from the start, the project was devised as an open-source, collaborative community project, with many experts involved over the years, including the Delft University of Technology and the consulting firm Accenture.[7]

Hennis broke this audacious goal into small milestones and started executing. He very quickly realized that he needed other specialists, including a coder, to create a platform for the project. Serendipitously, Hennis and a coder had crossed paths in meet-ups (an online platform that brings people with similar interests together), and during a two-day hackathon, and they had clicked immediately. "He knows about plants, electronics, and software, so he's a very good technical lead of the project," Hennis told me. He continued to build the team with other specialists over the years (biology, AI, and computer science experts, front-end developers, artists, hackers, business developers, product developers, and user experience designers).

He made contact through meetups and hackathons. Together, Hennis and the other team members built AstroPlant to inspire students, urban farmers, home gardeners, and other garden and plant enthusiasts to grow plants selected by the MELiSSA team.[8] AstroPlant kits include seeds provided by ESA and are distributed across the world, where users cultivate the plants under different environmental conditions.[9] The users record the environmental variables and pass these records to ESA partners, who then do research on plant models.[10] These models predict how plants behave under different circumstances, but the models have seldom been well validated.[11] The AstroPlant kit is used for validating the models, for rapid prototyping (quick experiments), and for building new protocols. Scientists need a wide range of conditions in the kits to create better mathematical models of plants and to ultimately be able to control their growth and performance.

As Hennis explained, the information will ultimately be used to speed up the design of a closed-loop artificial ecosystem able to sustain life. None of this work can happen without a community of people equally curious about the future of farming. AstroPlant hopes that understanding how plants respond to different conditions can eventually also help increase agricultural efficiency on earth. The technologies developed are used in controlled agriculture and, when sufficiently affordable, could provide food security in areas affected by severe weather events.

Like Hennis, you may have, in your curiosity journey, reached a point that requires other resources, including expertise outside your own, funding, technical assistance, and managerial help. It is certainly feasible to start your curiosity journey entirely on your own. However, somewhere along the way, you will most probably need to surround yourself with collaborators who can bring complementary skills to the table. I am mesmerized by biographies, movies, and documentaries about larger-than-life individuals who work alone in their garages and come out with flying cars; I am fascinated by detectives who, isolated in their quarters, solve impossible crimes. I want to cling to the romantic idea of the lone hero who overcomes unsurmountable obstacles and comes out a winner all on their own. But I also know that the majority of these stories apply to very few people. The reality is, we need a team to bring most ideas to fruition. Solving contemporary problems can be complex and demands technological sophistication and the collaboration of talented people.

What qualities should you look for in others who can dive off the cliff with you? How do you ensure that each member of your team is as inquisitive and passionate about the endeavor as you are? Start by looking for others who demonstrate the CURIOUS qualities described at the beginning of the book: people who are *collaborative*, *unabashedly* passionate about the subject, *resilient*, and *iconoclastic* and who have *outside* interests, feel an *urgency* to act, and *seek* surprises. Then, create a compelling message and a culture conducive to curiosity to ensure that each member becomes as curious and obsessed about the endeavor as you are.

THINKING OF GOING SOLO? THINK AGAIN.

There are three main reasons you should reconsider going solo: burnout, insufficient expertise, and giving in to giving up.

BURNOUT

As you get deeper into your curiosity journey, you will likely realize that there is more work to do than you can handle on your own. You have many questions that you can't an-swer and tasks that are beyond your skill set. Yet you have no one to share the work with or even to take on administrative tasks. The harsh reality is that embarking on a curiosity proj-ect, while deeply personal, can also become quite lonely. Our passion convinces us that no one can do the job as well as we can. But this attitude is a recipe for burnout. Going solo through rough patches means that we bear the stress ourselves. This sense of full responsibility taxes our physical and mental well-being, especially as we move outside our comfort zone.

INSUFFICIENT EXPERTISE

The major challenge of going solo on a curiosity journey, especially one centered on innovation, is that you have to depend on your own experience. Without partners or team-mates with sufficient expertise to back you up or fill in the gaps of your knowledge, you simply won't get very far.

GIVING IN TO GIVING UP

Investigative journalist Håkon Høydal told me that working with his partner, Einar Stangvik, helped him make much more progress than he would have on his own and that without that teamwork, he may have been tempted to give up during intense bouts of frustration. "Because we were two people, we were able to cheer each other on," he told me.[12] As with any challenge, there are highs and lows, triumphs and trib-ulations, and decisions to make. Sometimes we need the emotional and physical support a partner or team can offer. Working with others also gives us another reason to carry on: we don't want to let others down. Teammates help alleviate the occasional moments of boredom that happen when we are working on a project. In short, a bit of banter makes the whole journey feel lighter.

ASSEMBLING THE CURIOUS TEAM

Before you start searching for coconspirators, understand your own strengths and weaknesses. Yonatan Raz-Fridman, a successful serial entrepreneur, founded Kano Computing, a London-based start-up offering computers that kids can assemble themselves and then use to program software. He explains that you don't need to know everything about the area you're interested in; you just need to know where to fill in the blanks. "If you want to start a venture in AI," he says, "you don't need to be an expert in AI. Find an amazing scientist and entice them to be a part of it" to get to the bottom of the problem together.[13]

After becoming clear about where your knowledge gaps are, look to people you already know when you begin your search for people who have complementary skills. Reach out to your personal and professional contacts, and ask people in your networks whether they know someone with the expertise you need. Roberta Lucca, the previously mentioned cofounder of the award-winning London-based video game developer Bossa Studios, says it can be as simple as posting a message on your social media accounts: "Hey guys, does anyone know X kind of person? If so, please contact me."[14]

What follows are the crucial CURIOUS characteristics you need to look for when assembling a curiosity team.

Collaborative

Can they play well with others? Successful collaborations happen when there is a shared sense of purpose among team members. Look for people who have demonstrated the ability to work with others to find solutions to problems, who take responsibility for mistakes, who give credit where credit is due, and who actively listen to other team members. You also want to find people who are adaptive and organized and who can think for the long term.

Unabashedly Passionate About the Subject

Are they as interested as you are in the subject? Look for people who show a genuine interest in your project. But it's more than just shared interest. Passionate people have certain characteristics you should look for. Among these qualities are healthy self-confidence, perseverance, enthusiasm, positivity, and focus.

> *The reality is, we need a team to bring most ideas to fruition. Solving contemporary problems can be complex and demands technological sophistication and the collaboration of talented people.*

Resilient

Do they recover quickly from setbacks? The path to creating something that no one has ever accomplished before will be filled with a lot of roadblocks; you're going to experience a lot more failures than successes. Look for team members who exhibit natural resilience. How do they respond when things don't go as planned? How adaptable can they be? Look for people who have a strong core that allows them to persist through all the hardships that emerge along the way.

Iconoclastic

Are they independent thinkers? Look for people who are comfortable challenging the status quo. Find mavericks who know how to tell others what they may not necessarily want to hear. Look for team members who can ask a series of difficult questions and challenge assumptions.

Open to Outside Interests

Do they have side gigs or hobbies? The best collaborators are those whose inquisitiveness about life and the world around them doesn't come as a sense of duty but is genuine. Good collaborators don't wear blinders. Team members should have interests or hobbies and can draw connections between those activities and the work they are doing for you.

Urgent

Do they feel a sense of urgency to get things done? Look for people who have demonstrated success in executing the tasks necessary to develop ideas. Can-do people often have street smarts along with professional skills and experience. People who get things done know how to compromise—a big part of successful collaboration. They don't engage in office politics and gossip. People who get things done are also driven to see progress and help others do the same. For them, problems are a chance to innovate.

Surprise Seeking

Do they embrace the unknown? Find collaborators who enjoy trying new things and don't have fixed ideas about a range of topics. New ideas and experiences draw them in. These people know that there is always more to learn.

MAKING THE MISSION THE MESSAGE

You also need to create a compelling message and a culture conducive to curiosity to ensure that you can sustain the team's interest. Clearly communicating your story is crucial to getting the best from your team. Ben Saunders, the British polar explorer, says his team had a definite shared sense of purpose, and each member understood what they were trying to do.[15] A team of eight people were working toward making sure that Saunders and fellow explorer, Tarka L'Herpiniere, would break the record for the longest-ever polar journey on foot from the edge of the Antarctic Continent to the South Pole and back—a journey of around eighteen hundred miles (twenty-nine hundred kilometers), which took them 108 days to complete. "I think we all shared this sense of excitement that it had never been done before," Saunders said.[16] The other important factor was that Saunders's team members felt that they were working toward a common goal that they understood and believed. That's where an effective pitch comes in. Passion and fire engage people and encourage them to think big early on.

Spread your enthusiasm by painting a compelling and purposeful picture of how things could be in the future, and make that picture relevant. To create an effective pitch, keep these tips in mind:

1. People remember stories, not data. Don't flood prospective collaborators with too many numbers—instead, weave the data points and facts into a narrative. The chances that they will remember the salient details are greater if they hear the information in an engaging story.
2. Increase excitement and buy-in by building drama and making the story exciting through surprising details and unexpected outcomes.

3. Make sure the story you tell is relatable to your audience. You have to know whom you are talking to and tailor the story to their interests and skill sets.

> Perhaps the most important lesson is that a fine balancing act is required to nurture a culture of curiosity.

NURTURING A CULTURE OF CURIOSITY

Once you have assembled a committed CURIOUS team, turn your attention to establishing a strong culture of curiosity. A culture is the glue that binds everyone together along the journey. Develop an environment that celebrates discovery and questions, where curiosity is a habit. Your aim should be to create an environment that turns lifelong learning into the team's lifestyle.

Bizarrely, people often go out of their way to attract team members with inquisitive mindsets and then put them in environments where curiosity is discouraged. Psychology professor Todd Kashdan found something puzzling: Although 84 percent of respondents said their employer encourages curiosity, 60 percent report that their employer has erected barriers that discourage its expression.[17] "They cling to legacy structures and systems that emphasize authority over inquiry and routine over resourcefulness," Kashdan said in the *Harvard Business Review*.[18] Too often, our obsession with efficiency makes us stop asking questions as we believe we already have all the answers.

So, what can we do about it? We can embrace three key contradictions: Stretching beyond the comfort zone involves feeling comfortable, humility requires boldness, and celebrating team cohesion entails taking diverse points into account. Pulling too far on one side can prove counterproductive. For instance, excessive cohesiveness can lead to groupthink—the phenomenon in which pressure to follow others overrides our ability to objectively consider other opinions and contribute novel ideas. Ultimately, groupthink increases the risk of poor group decision-making.[19] Perhaps the most important lesson is that a fine balancing act is required to nurture a culture of curiosity.

Encourage Comfort in Stretch

Fashion designer Mary Katrantzou was born in Athens, Greece, and initially attended the Rhode Island School of Design, in Providence, to pursue a bachelor's degree in architecture.[20] Her degree offered a semester at another university abroad. The only course that was available in London, where she wanted to be, was one in textile design at Central Saint Martins (CSM).[21] Seduced by the opportunity to channel her talent in a different creative field, Katrantzou made the leap and fully transferred to CSM. "I had heard so much about Louise Wilson, the professor who runs the MA [master of art] in fashion course and the incredible people who had come out of the course," she told me.[22] Katrantzou was so successful in the course, her fashion design work was chosen to open the CSM graduate show.

"Naively, after I finished my master's, I applied for NewGen funding from the British Fashion Council," she said. "I got the sponsorship and put together fifteen shift dresses not really believing that they would generate sales."[23] They were a hit. Katrantzou launched her eponymous fashion label in London in 2008 and has since received several prestigious awards. Her work has been exhibited at the New York Metropolitan Museum of Art and the Victoria and

Albert Museum in London. Her designs have been worn by the likes of Beyoncé, Michelle Obama, and Naomi Campbell and are carried by more than one hundred retailers around the globe.[24]

To maintain the curiosity and enthusiasm of her team, Katrantzou constantly asks questions, challenges herself and the team members, and plays devil's advocate for anything the team voices. "It's a very democratic approach in terms of questioning everything, and I think it leads to meaningful conversations," she said.[25]

Other entrepreneurs agree with the notion that stretching boundaries makes dynamic teams. Sam Bompas, from the London-based avant-garde experiential food company Bompas & Parr, told me, "The things my team will say they are most proud of are the bits that they have literally been crying in the studio about or when they said, 'This is too much. I can't do anymore.' Six months later, they will say those difficult challenges are the ones they care the most about. Over time, we're trying to grow everyone, so giving them more difficult projects within a framework where they feel stretched but not overly pressured is key so that they don't get bored or become so stressed that they leave. Luckily, I am in a team that is small enough that I can speak to everyone and find out what they are working on, and how they are doing with it."[26]

There is a thin line between challenging people and creating a culture of fear and insecurity. Team members must feel challenged by their working environment but not threatened by the fear of losing control. The level of uncertainty that surrounds curious teams must be counterbalanced by encouragement for them to gradually develop a belief in themselves and their work. They must feel safe.

Moving between the worlds of improv and sketch comedy and planetary exploration motivated Jon Wiley, who studied theater (with an astronomy minor) at the University of Texas and who was interested in web design.[27] He pushed himself to see how he could combine the tools and perspectives that are used in theater with the scientific exploration and experimentation that happens in software engineering. Wiley honed his web design skills over the course of several projects. Armed with a unique set of skills and experiences, he convinced Google to hire him in 2006.[28] As a result, he became the first designer for Google AutoComplete and has led several teams (e.g., leading the Search UX team and co-founding the augmented reality/VR team in 2014). "Google is a place that supports curiosity," Wiley said, "even if the act of chasing down some of the answers isn't fruitful. You need to focus your resources and motivate people to be curious, by not punishing them for going down the wrong path." Developing a safe environment, where people know that failure is an inherent part of curiosity and are supported when they experiment with new techniques, is key to building your team's confidence.

> *In any demanding endeavor,*
> *curiosity is not an individual act—*
> *its results rely heavily on social*
> *interaction and collective inspiration.*

Embrace Bold Humility

Humility helps teams realize what they don't know. What do the movies *Aladdin*, *The Jungle Book*, and *Harry Potter* all have in common? Each of them enjoyed the touch of Ceylan Shevket, the blockbuster visual effects artist. Shevket has been involved in these and many other movies and helped filmmakers bring their visions to life. Working with her teams in different companies, Shevket animated myriad visual effects, including imaginary creatures, dynamic crowd simulations, and attention-grabbing scenes of destruction.

"We surround ourselves and hire people from different specialities," Shevket told me. "Our one department, even though it is specialist, brings in people who are disciplined in model making, special effects, and other areas. We all learn from each other, in an environment that is as collaborative as possible, so when there was a new technique or a new way of approaching something, we try and teach everybody else."[29]

Curious teams are humble about what they don't know. They invite experts to update or train them in relation to the latest developments in their fields. They also take turns. In some meetings, they teach, while in others, they learn. Being boldly humble helps curious and collaborative teams learn more.

Curiosity flourishes in environments where bold humility is modeled and encouraged. And that's the point: curious cultures believe that humility makes us recognize what we need to know in a constantly changing world and drives us to be bold, to act, and to stand up for what we believe in.

Cultivate Cohesive Diversity

Building a culture of curiosity is about recognizing the value of diverse perspectives. Create a culture that doesn't just welcome diversity but also actively champions and facilitates it. Instead of seeking out those who live in similar bubbles (the same background, perspective, environment, etc.), look for people who bring different experiences, backgrounds, opinions, and approaches.

Diversity helps with another challenge that we often face on our collaborative curiosity journeys: The team's inquisitiveness levels may drop over time. In the beginning, the shiny curiosity object feels novel and exciting. But once the novelty starts wearing off, we wonder where our spark went. Team members may disengage; they may stop asking questions, and idea generation may suffer.

Pete Bottomley, the cofounder and game designer of White Paper Games, an award-winning game development studio based in

Manchester, England, explained how diversity can nourish curiosity. In the games his company designs, the players assume different roles and explore wonderfully crafted worlds with optional puzzle solving. Developing video games is not for the faint of heart. It takes on average three to four years to move from concept to market release.[30] Bottomley is passionate about building diverse teams because they create more exciting, layered games. The company's team of experts who represent a variety of backgrounds and experiences didn't happen by chance. It was the outcome of team curation, of choosing members who not only brought different skills but also brought in different cultural and social milieus.[31]

Bompas says he sponsors cultural trips and encourages his team members to share new experiences on WhatsApp groups. These practices rekindle sparks of learning and curiosity.[32] Interestingly, psychology professor Arthur Aron from the State University of New York at Stony Brook and his colleagues found that couples who engaged in more-exciting activities together feel less bored in their relationships than do couples who engage in activities more routine, and the less-bored couples rate their relationships as having better quality.[33] Working on challenging tasks alongside other people who bring in new perspectives seems to help in long-term endeavors, where keeping interest alive proves harder. The same can be said of entrepreneurial teams.

Giampaolo Dallara, a legend in motorsports, was born in Parma, Italy. He caught the car-racing bug at a young age when his dad would take him along in car and motorbike races.[34] Dallara attended the Polytechnic University of Milan, where he studied naval engineering.[35] At the time, in the early 1960s, the automaker Ferrari was looking for bright graduates, and one of Dallara's professors was approached by Enzo Ferrari and asked if he had any student worthy of joining the company.[36] The professor recommended Dallara. He joined Ferrari in a heartbeat, turning his dream to work in the race-car industry into reality. After Ferrari, Dallara worked for the racing team of Maserati and Lamborghini, where he designed the chassis for the iconic Miura, and then for De Tomaso, another Italian carmaker. While he was working for others, his desire to create something of his own was growing stronger. In 1972, Dallara took a huge step forward and founded his own company, Dallara Automobili da Competizione, in the garage behind his house.

Over the years, Dallara and his company became synonymous with races all over the world. Dallara and his team worked painstakingly to design and construct race cars and road vehicles, and in 2017, they launched the company's first-ever street-legal two-seater sports car, the Dallara Stradale, and opened the Dallara Academy, an educational center to train young people in aeronautic engineering.

"I am lucky to have a small racetrack nearby that hosts the Formula SAE, which gathers eighty universities from twenty-five countries, each presenting potentially disruptive ideas. That reminds us all how much is left to do," Dallara told me.[37] "There are a few gurus who I occasionally engage with in search of feedback. However, I believe that young talent adds freshness to my experience, and their perspective can be beneficial," he added. Dallara and others like him credit their success on combining experience with fresh ways of thinking.

Although curiosity requires diversity and autonomy, one problem with diverse teams is that they may not speak the same language. One way to alleviate this discrepancy is to always ensure that members are aligned around the mission and understand the common goals. Raia Hadsell, the previously discussed senior research scientist from Google, said that at DeepMind Technologies, a British subsidiary of Google, the culture is centered around working together toward a common purpose.

On May 29, 1953, Sir Edmund Hillary and Tenzing Norgay reached the summit of Mount Everest.[38] Colonel John Hunt, the mastermind behind the Everest expedition, knew that to reach the summit, he needed a superb team. Selecting the right people and making them feel they were embarking on a worthwhile mission became his top priorities. The expedition team members were chosen for their mountaineering skills as well as their hungry, urgent minds. The team was consciously diverse and included a student, a statistician, schoolmasters, physicians, a physiologist, a soldier, an apiarist, a journalist, and Sherpa guides.[39] Hunt asked his team to channel their curiosity and learn everything that they could in their respective fields in relation to the ascent to Mount Everest. He also asked his team members to share everything with each other. Hunt wanted to make everyone feel involved, as if they all had a stake in the project. The selected few had to spend as much time as possible together before the iconic journey. They all had to attend meetings at the Royal Geographic Society and extensive field trips in Snowdonia, Wales.[40] The expedition was a success, thanks to the diverse team.

Assembling and nourishing a dream team is fundamental to reaching significant goals. Curiosity projects start with a vision and only become realized fully when there is a strong team involved.

Successfully recruiting the right team, creating a compelling message, and building the right culture takes practice. You may not get it right, and you may have to tweak the makeup of your team. People will also leave, or you will have to let them go. There's no shame in that; you may have erred, but missteps can be redirected and corrected. Changing course doesn't make you weak or inferior—quite the opposite. Owning up to mistakes and fixing them gains you more trust and respect from the team in the long run. In any demanding endeavor, curiosity is not an individual act—its results rely heavily on social interaction and collective inspiration.

– THE TAKEAWAYS –

- There are three reasons to create a team around your curiosity project: burnout, insufficient expertise, and giving in to giving up.
- Assembling the dream team is about hiring CURIOUS people:
  - » Collaborative
  - » Unabashedly passionate about the subject
  - » Resilient
  - » Iconoclastic
  - » Open to outside interests
  - » Urgent
  - » Surprise seeking

- To ensure that each member becomes as curious and obsessed about the endeavor as you are, follow these steps:
  - » Make sure you have a compelling message.
  - » Nurture a culture of curiosity that involves embracing three key contradictions: comfort with stretching, bold humility, and cohesive diversity.

SIX

Get Ready

> One man cannot practice many arts with success.
>
> —PLATO

BEN SAUNDERS AND TARKA L'HERPINIERE, BRITISH POLAR EXPLORERS and ultra-endurance athletes we met earlier, set out from Ross Island on October 26, 2013. Their goal was bold: to be the first to complete a return journey from Ross Island, off the continent of Antarctica, to the South Pole using the same route attempted by Sir Ernest Shackleton on the Nimrod Expedition in 1907–1909 and by Robert Falcon Scott on the Terra Nova Expedition in 1910–1913.[1] After all, Shackleton's attempt is often referred to as a "successful failure," and Scott and his men never returned from their journey; they died on the return trip.[2]

Saunders's mother had never been happy about his career path and was more stressed than ever about his upcoming expedition.[3] Out of the nine attempts to walk from Ross Island to the South Pole and back, nobody had ever made it, and five had died in the process.[4] No one had tried the trek after the challenge had defeated Shackleton and Scott. The entire journey was around eighteen hundred miles (twenty-nine hundred kilometers). Saunders and L'Herpiniere were not trying to find out where the South Pole was. That had been discovered a long time ago. They wanted to see if the journey itself could be completed. "We were trying to go further than anyone had ever gone on foot, in the toughest place on earth," Saunders told me. "We were definitely exploring in a human sense, and we were definitely going to be in completely uncharted territory in the human sense as well. We were trying to go a thousand kilometers further than anyone had ever walked before in these conditions, so there was a definite step into the unknown in that respect."[5] For years, he had been pitching this journey as the ultimate ultra-endurance challenge.

Saunders grew up in the southwest of England, in Devon and Somerset. With his younger brother, he spent a lot of time outdoors, exploring nearby woods and climbing trees.[6] They were active boys, adventurous and inquisitive. "I learned through attempt and experience, and that's what adventure and exploration are about," Saunders added. Reading stories about trailblazers and mountaineers in *National Geographic* as a boy also caught his imagination and helped solidify his fascination with exploration. In his teens, he became involved with cycling, running, and endurance sports. He was intrigued by the functional element. "The concept of having a goal and the consistent application of effort through training, repetition, persistence, and focus to improve your performance intrigued me," Saunders noted. Endurance sports, which are mainly about demanding preparation, consistency, and goal setting, ultimately tied in with his aspiration to one day embark on his own expeditions.

After attending the Royal Military Academy Sandhurst, Saunders went straight into exploration. He was twenty-three when he attempted to reach the North Pole from Russia. He joined Arctic explorer and ocean conservationist Rupert Nigel Pendrill "Pen"

Hadow in this quest. It was a two-man, unsupported expedition (they used no external help like the wind, animals, or a motor to raise their speed or to help them with the load they were carrying).[7] After fifty-nine days into the excursion, Saunders and Hadow had to give up because of dangerous weather conditions.[8] "We didn't get to the North Pole; it was a failure," Saunders told me.[9] Despite failing to reach their intended destination, the expedition kicked off his adventurous career path. The more Saunders learned about the expedition and exploration field, the more he became interested in iconic journeys that had yet to be completed. The longest and most arduous of all was, of course, the one that he started with L'Herpiniere on October 26, 2013. There was a definite learning curve. "There were ten expeditions leading up to that one," Saunders told me. "And each one was a stepping-stone or a prototype in some ways."

Purposeful curiosity helps us understand that big visions are not executed overnight. To reach a goal, you have to make a long-term commitment that requires planning, dedication, patience, and the ability to avoid distractions. Saunders and his team threw themselves into preparing for this demanding trip. Antarctica is an extraordinary place of extremes. It is the coldest, windiest, driest, highest place on earth. It is twice the size of Australia. "There's no Antarctic rescue service," Saunders added. "So if you're doing something risky, like walking across it, and there's the potential that you might need rescuing if you become injured or ill or whatever, then you must create that safety net yourself. You must have aircraft in Antarctica, you must have the communications, you must have the ability to share your position automatically. It took a lot of figuring out, so, yes, we spent a long time thinking about contingency planning by imagining what would be the worst that could happen. We asked, 'What are the challenging situations that we're likely to get into, and then how can we manage those?' We had to ensure that we had aircraft, people, and expertise ready to go. It was a lot of work."[10]

Saunders and L'Herpiniere reached the South Pole on December 26, 2013, and completed their expedition back at Ross Island on February 7, 2014. It was a record-breaking expedition, an eighteen-hundred-mile round-trip journey on foot from the edge of Antarctica to the South Pole, and back. To date, it is the longest human journey ever, a camping trip that lasted 108 days and that took Saunders about ten months to recover from.[11]

There comes a time to stop talking and start doing. You probably aren't going to decide to launch a polar expedition, but you may well be confronted with many life-changing decisions, such as leaving your job to launch a business or organizing a trip that demands physical and mental strength. "You can't just hitchhike to Antarctica on the spur of the moment," Saunders said. "It takes planning and work, a lot of very boring work. Curiosity is part of that equation, but it's not the only thing. There's got to be a willingness to put in the work required as well."[12]

There are three common problems that can get in the way of preparations for your journey: inability to predict all outcomes, the planning fallacy, and the thirst for instant gratification.

> *Purposeful curiosity helps us understand that big visions are not executed overnight. To reach a goal, you have to make a long-term commitment that requires planning, dedication, patience, and the ability to avoid distractions.*

INABILITY TO PREDICT ALL OUTCOMES

Becoming comfortable with moving forward when we don't know exactly what is coming our way is tricky, to say the least. Realizing that our new curiosity projects may not be based on intuition or experience will overwhelm many of us. It's easy for fear to creep in if we don't know what's going to play out. Challenges pop up when we least expect them. How do we prepare mentally and physically for things that we haven't done or that nobody else has done before? How can we accurately predict possible problems and their solutions, especially when there are few (or no) previous examples to draw on? To make matters worse, those who have successfully completed unusual curiosity journeys (an expedition no one had completed before, starting an unusual business in an unknown market, manufacturing a completely new device or tool) often say that they felt stymied when their predictable, ordered, and scheduled lives were replaced by a series of unpredictable events.

PLANNING FALLACY

The old adage about home renovations—they cost more and take longer than you think—is true for curiosity journeys. Most of us underestimate the time and the cost of our preparations and the journey itself; this underestimation is also known as the *planning fallacy*. Research from professors Roger Buehler of the Wilfrid Laurier University, Dale Griffin of the University of British Columbia, and Michael Ross of the University of Waterloo shows that the planning fallacy is a common problem. In one study, they assessed the accuracy of the estimates that psychology students made of the time they would need to complete their honors thesis.[13] Interestingly, 70 percent of the students took longer than they had predicted—on average, seven days longer than their worst-case forecast (forty-eight days) and twenty-two days longer than their seemingly realistic estimate (thirty-three days).

Even experienced planners are susceptible to the planning fallacy. In 2004, Raphaël Domjan, the previously mentioned eco-explorer, conceived an outlandish idea—to circumnavigate the globe aboard a ship powered entirely by solar energy. First, Domjan had to make sure that his dream was even possible. He asked an engineering school to do a feasibility study of potential routes and a solar boatbuilding company to prototype, on paper, a vessel that could sustain such an adventure. He also had to find the funds to make the boat and the trip a reality. After four years of searching, Domjan convinced a German businessman to finance the project. Then, it took him another year to do all the studies necessary before building a catamaran. Nineteen more months were spent constructing the largest solar-power boat ever built.[14]

PlanetSolar, the 115-foot catamaran, was made of durable, lightweight carbon material and was covered with thirty-eight thousand solar cells that fed power to six blocks of lithium-ion batteries.[15] The catamaran, led by French Captain Patrick Marchesseau and its four crew members, including Domjan, set out from Monaco on September 27, 2010, heading west and across the Atlantic Ocean. The voyage took them 584 days, roughly nineteen months, to make it all around the world at a maximum speed of ten knots and an average speed of five knots, using only power harvested from the sun. Domjan's curiosity journey took around six years to plan and a year and a half to accomplish, at a cost of nearly $17 million.[16] There was no way that Domjan could have predicted those kinds of costs when he started planning the trip.

THIRST FOR INSTANT GRATIFICATION

Whether it is the latest mobile phone, a tempting cupcake, or a piece of information, we want it right now. We live in a get-it-now world. Some of us may compress the preparation phase so severely because we want a quick rush of adrenaline. Or we believe that we lack the time or the necessary resources such as financing and materials, and so we rush into the project. We may even convince ourselves that we can launch without preparing. But curiosity journeys require substantial preparation. To mentally prepare for the unexpected, we must learn to delay gratification. If we are curious about something, we should refrain from going into action mode straightaway, without a second thought. We need to develop a rational and coolheaded insight into the best way forward and how to take calculated risks. In this way, we balance the risks and decide what we are comfortable with. As polar explorer Felicity Aston said, "It's a process that takes years. Satisfying some of this curiosity is certainly not something that comes easy and quickly. You have to be prepared that it might take two or three years of your life before you get these answers."[17] Favoring short-term gains over long-term advances is not an ally of adequate preparation.

> *Learning to delay gratification is an essential part of mental preparation for the unexpected.*

THE POWER OF ANALOG EXPLORATION

Mindful of these three problems, prepare for your curiosity journeys by leveraging the power of analog exploration: capturing parts of what your journey might be like in an environment that resembles the wild or the actual environment you'll soon be in. We cannot prepare for everything; time, money, equipment, and access to helpers or staff will often pose constraints. Analog exploration enables us to explore in a quicker and less expensive way. It is a form of personalized risk assessment designed to recognize problems and figure out either how to prevent them or how to cope with them if they emerge. It trains us to our maximum potential while reducing the chances of unwanted setbacks, which could cost us the success of our curiosity journey. The success of the analog exploration program depends on both our commitment and our ability to execute it well, keeping in mind that periodic evaluation is key to reformulate the program as our needs evolve with consistent practice.

The purpose of analog exploration is threefold. First, it acts as a testing ground for the physical demands or mental strength, or both, required to pursue the challenge. Any signs of quitting here would spell disaster for the actual curiosity journey. Second, a successful analog exploration helps us gradually build a reputation around the domain and meet other like-minded people. Third, this type of exploration makes us stronger, more confident, and more knowledgeable about the situations that we will experience. Rehearsing our journeys forces us to come up with backup systems or procedures.

In an ideal world, analog exploration is a three-stage process. First, you start by imagining the journey, being curious about its hurdles and possible solutions, on paper. Then, you further explore these hurdles and solutions by conducting experiments (in labs, garages, or anywhere else you can). Last, if you can, you approximate reality in a natural setting with deliberate practice and controlled explorations.

Be Curious About Problems and Solutions on Paper

Curiosity about what may lie ahead is a critical part of the preparation for curiosity journeys. Kick off your analog preparation by imagining what the journey is likely to look like and figuring out possible solutions to challenges you foresee. Do it on paper: conduct a premortem (i.e., imagine a few what-if scenarios) and come back from the future.

Conduct a Premortem

Think through all possible problems to focus your preparation. Gary Klein, an expert on decision-making, introduces the premortem method in a *Harvard Business Review* article.[18] Think of this method as the opposite of a postmortem. A postmortem allows people to extract lessons about what worked and what went wrong in a project. Naturally, only future projects benefit from a postmortem. On the contrary, a premortem, where people can spot possible problems at the beginning of a project and seek solutions, focuses on improving current projects (rather than learning from their autopsies). Klein explains that teams performing premortems imagine that their project has failed and focus on unpacking what could have gone wrong.[19]

In a single, powerful statement, Aston summed up how she goes about a premortem: "You have to assume that every bit of kit you have may break or go wrong at some point."[20]

Purposefully curious people use the premortem method and assume that the "patient" has died. They ask themselves, "What will I do? And how will I work it out?" They then collate all the problems that they have identified and try to find solutions. Using their insights, they fill gaps. In some cases, it may take a long time to fill the gaps with worthy answers—but patience and perseverance are the keys to success in this part of the journey. You can also ask yourself a lot of what-ifs and only stop asking when you're happy with the answers.

Thieme Hennis, who is coordinating the AstroPlant project discussed earlier, pointed out that when he works on something new, he starts by writing down a couple of scenarios, or how a system he has imagined would work.[21] He then notes these scenarios in a spreadsheet and goes through them step-by-step to identify any problems. After several iterations, he develops a working model. The objective is to anticipate the future, assess different risks, intimately know every aspect of the plan, and identify answers. While you cannot eliminate all the risks, you can continue to explore ways to mitigate problems. You can consider ways to reduce risks so that you're at least comfortable moving forward, confident you have the tools to fix difficulties as they arise.

Come Back from the Future

To apply the come-back-from-the-future approach, ask yourself what the best possible future could be and then work out the milestones you have to reach to get there. Start with a clear endpoint—what you want to achieve—and then work backward from there to try to unpack everything that will make your goal possible and everything that will make it improbable. Peter Beck, the previously introduced New Zealand engineer and founder and CEO of Rocket Lab, explained to me how this works in practice: "All the things that make [a journey] improbable need to be mitigated, and then all the things that make it possible, you need to knock off one by one."[22] Working backward from the desired endpoint gives you objectives for this day, this week, this month. This stepwise approach can make you curious about what you need to learn and who has done it in the past. Ceylan Shevket, the blockbuster visual effects artist, advised asking, "What do I want to know, and who currently do I know who is similar to where I want to be? Ask that person how they got there, what knowledge they have, and work backwards."[23]

Further Explore Hurdles and Solutions by Conducting Experiments

After you've spent time preparing on paper, start building a program of experiments. Claudia Pasquero, an associate professor in architecture at the Bartlett School of Architecture at UCL, landscape architecture professor at Innsbruck University, and the cofounder of the London-based ecoLogicStudio, is a pioneer in bio-architecture. That's the study of how living microorganisms can synthesize materials that can grow in buildings. Pasquero's work and research operates at the intersection of biology, computation, and design. Much of the work that she and her cofounder, Marco Poletto, do is based on years of experimentation. "I do my experiments," Pasquero told me enthusiastically. "I take many photos to see how the biology elements develop."[24] Often, these experiments happen in the lab. "I like to know exactly all the parameters, and I want to work in a lab where there is no temperature change, no movement, no pressure change, and I want to have total control all the time on the experiment," she notes. Pasquero and Poletto will also observe how microalgae evolve on an architectural structure where there is interaction with humans and real conditions like changing weather.[25]

In your own experiments, you can run frequent mini-simulations to expose potential pitfalls. Conduct experiments to anticipate where problems are likely. This work is complex and requires a relentless attitude with simulations often running several times a day and six days a week. Raia Hadsell, the senior research scientist at Google DeepMind, told me during our conversation, "A nice thing about being in Google is that we have a lot of computational resources. I can launch a lot of experiments very easily; it's just about writing code and having a machine to run that on, and Google really supports that."[26]

Resist the urge to start digging in immediately. Stand back and ask, "What are the right questions to ask? What are the right problems to go after?" Focus on articulating the relevant questions; otherwise your research may not meet your objectives. Develop hypotheses about how solutions may play out, and test them, in labs, garages, anywhere you can.

Try to impose a variety of constraints in your experiments to focus your exploration. Beck told me how important it is to have a laser-like focus on a very few priorities while experimenting with hurdles and solutions. At Rocket Lab, people spend enough time asking questions about what's important; they define the lab's greatest priorities, now and in the future, and use data as the tool, rather than the driver, for exploration. They use artificial deadlines to keep track of their progress and, if necessary, take corrective actions or go into new directions. Rocket Lab people are curious to see what will happen, whether their hypotheses will be proven true. They conduct experiments to test whether the idea was any good and if there is any interest in the idea.

Results of your curiosity experiments may generate all kinds of interesting ideas. ecoLogicStudio, for instance, developed a carbon-neutral living biocurtain designed to be hung from the side of a building. The feature produces oxygen by using microalgae to capture one kilogram of carbon dioxide per day (the equivalent of twenty large trees) from polluted air.[27]

Just as physical strength takes months of training, so does painstaking mental preparation.

Approximate Reality with Deliberate Practice in Natural Settings

When we feel ready, it is time to progress into the practice zone, in an environment that goes beyond the lab and captures what it is like to live and operate in the wild. The practice zone should feel challenging but within reach of our comfort zone. Initially we may feel as if practice punishes us. Training for something in a natural setting, whether that's a mountain, our garage, or an art studio, can be grueling. When we practice, our heart rate increases, stimulating our limbic system (the part of the brain that senses hazard, which tells us to stop).

We must accept that deliberate practice is a challenging process but that the reward is moving closer to our goal. However, with time, everything becomes easier. The boost we get from endorphins is an extra benefit. Testing the waters is possibly the most difficult part, so it is important to be patient.

Train Like a Spartan Warrior

The preparation that you go through while preparing for a curiosity journey reminds me of the Spartans' brutal training. By practicing regularly, these warriors improved their stamina and pushed themselves to the limit. We should do the same to prepare for our curiosity journeys. At some point, we must force ourselves to do the things that we don't want to do. Nicole Cooke, the British Olympic gold medalist, shared some pivotal advice her father gave her: "Rather than just accepting the way things are, if you actually went out and worked and trained for something, you could improve."[28]

Talking to Chen Reiss, the Israeli soprano who has awed the world with her voice, I realized how much time, work, and effort training entails. She has a tight schedule, based entirely around work and family demands, and she follows it with military-like precision. "When I start a new part, I'm full volume, so full speed, just day and night, studying the text, studying the music," she told me.[29] Curious people roll up their sleeves and go for it. There are no hacks in training. "Singing is like being an athlete," Reiss explained. "Maybe you can understand the principles of singing, but unless you practice every day, you lose it. So, you absolutely have to be at it. Otherwise, you're not in shape and you just cannot perform." No marathon runner ever steps up to the start line in a big race without putting in the training miles. They practice for months, if not years. They schedule the training needed to achieve their goals. "You have to feel very secure in what you do," Reiss added. "And what gives you the feeling of security is the practice and the study and the preparation."

Train the Mind for the Unexpected

Just as physical strength takes months of training, so does the painstaking mental preparation. The curiosity journeys that we will embark on may have many variables that cannot be predicted. Sometimes, there won't be solid answers. We need to train our minds to cope with not knowing—with that sense of the unexpected while keeping the prize in mind. As Saunders put it, "I think you can plan up to a certain point, but you also have to be aware that you are going into a very unpredictable environment. In some ways, you have to plan for uncertainty, and you have to be prepared for uncertainty and be flexible."[30]

A lot of mental prep is actually physical. Regularly doing things you don't want to do teaches self-discipline and builds mental resilience. The good news is that by putting ourselves in challenging situations, we activate our mental strength and boost our loyalty to our purpose.

An analog environment, one that resembles the natural setting where your journey will take place, is important but isn't always possible or practical. When Aston was preparing a team of women for the Arctic, she decided to take them to the desert in Oman to train. "The reason the training there was so successful was because when we set out each day, those dunes, that terrain, couldn't be accurately mapped," she said. "We did not know how far we'd be able to travel that day, how long it might take us. We didn't know how many dunes we'd have to go up and over. We didn't know how we were going to navigate precisely through that terrain. As a result, we had to make decisions as challenges occurred, in real time. It was very immediate. That's very much like the Arctic Ocean, where everything's moving. You don't know what you're going to come across in a day, you don't know how far you're going to be able to travel, how far you're going to go."[31]

While it may be painful to resist an urge in the moment, sacrificing an immediate want for a later larger reward pays off. Reiss told me during our conversation how she has to sacrifice an evening out or going to an opera for listening to the music she has to learn. "Once you make up your mind, then the opera house or the orchestra, they construct a very clear schedule, and that helps. When I just start to learn a role, it's a very long process. It takes sometimes one year to learn a role. It depends how complicated it is, musically."[32] The weeks, months, or years of planning, training, and sacrificing and the desire to reach a destination are what make the curiosity journey possible and worth the effort.

– THE TAKEAWAYS –

- Meticulous preparation and relentless training bring out our confidence in embarking on our curiosity journeys.
- Three problems can get in the way of our preparations:
  » *Inability to predict all outcomes:* We fail to properly prepare physically and mentally for things that we haven't done or that nobody else has done before.
  » *The planning fallacy:* We underestimate the time and the cost needed for our preparation.
  » *The thirst for instant gratification:* We are hardwired for instant gratification.

- We can optimize the journeys before launch by using analog exploration. Analog exploration is about capturing parts of what our curiosity journey is likely to be when we go into the wild.
- Fueled by curiosity, analog exploration happens either on paper or in the wild. On paper, try these approaches:
  - » Conduct premortems.
  - » Imagine what-if scenarios, and only stop when you are happy with the answers.
  - » Adopt a come-back-from-the-future approach. Start by setting a clear endpoint—what you want to achieve—and then work backward from there to unpack everything that will make the endpoint possible (and everything that will make it improbable).

- In the wild, try these approaches to analog exploration:
  - » *In labs or garages:* From our observations in these controlled environments, we develop hypotheses and experiments to test how the solution may play out.
  - » *By approximating reality:* We deliberately practice physically and mentally in smaller or controlled natural settings. One hallmark of curious people is that they don't leap into the unknown until they have practiced. They take meticulous notes and rehearse moves over and over. It may take them several weeks, months, or even years of preparation before they feel ready.

- Before you go into the wild, look at everything. Identify potential problems, and devise ways to mitigate them. For problems you can't manage, accept them and embark on the journey anyway.

SEVEN

Leap into the Unknown

> *If it's a good idea, go ahead and do it. It is much*
> *easier to apologize than it is to get permission.*
>
> —ADMIRAL GRACE HOPPER, *BUILT TO LEARN*

CHARLES GORDON-LENNOX, THE 11TH DUKE OF RICHMOND, LEN-
nox, Gordon, and Aubigny, first became interested in photography
when he was ten years old and at Eton College, a prestigious independent boarding school founded in 1440 in Windsor, England.[1]
Eton has taught princes and prime ministers, including Prince William and Boris Johnson; writers, such as George Orwell and Ian
Fleming; and actors, including Hugh Laurie and Damian Lewis.[2] In
the early 1970s, Gordon-Lennox's insatiable passion for photography prompted him to drop out of Eton at sixteen and enter the film
and photography world. At the time, the renowned filmmaker Stan-
ley Kubrick was looking for a preproduction stills photographer
for the 1975 film *Barry Lyndon*. Gordon-Lennox managed to get the
job and spent the next year and a half working with Kubrick and
Sir Kenneth Adam (an Oscar-winning production designer).[3] This

invaluable experience at a young age influenced Gordon-Lennox's future career as an award-winning advertising photographer in London, with clients including Levi's (a US clothing company) and Imperial Chemical Industries (a British chemical company).[4]

In the early 1990s, when Gordon-Lennox was thirty-nine, his father handed him the reins of the twelve-thousand-acre Goodwood Estate in West Sussex.[5] He moved with his family from London into the main house and very soon realized that farming, woodland management, and the periodic income from horse racing were not enough to keep the estate afloat. He became curious about potential new ideas that could generate additional revenues quickly. Working alongside his father, he immersed himself in the business of the estate, delving deeply into his family history in the process.[6] He went through family photographs, estate archives, and family-related books his parents had sent him when he was at Eton College.

His research took him back in time to another important tradition associated with Goodwood, motorsport.[7] His grandfather, Frederick Charles Gordon-Lennox, 9th Duke of Richmond, had, despite resistance from his family, become a racing driver, an automotive and aeronautical engineer, and a motor-racing promoter.[8] Passionate about Goodwood and motorsport, Frederick ran casual sporting events for car enthusiasts on the property, but his vision was to convert the road around the airfield of the estate to a great racetrack after the war. He opened the Goodwood circuit in 1948, where Sir Stirling Moss won his first single-seater race.[9] The racetrack continued to host racing events until the mid-1960s. The family decided to close it in 1966, when the course could no longer accommodate the constantly evolving sport.[10] The circuit remained in a semi-dormant state for the next thirty years.

"I tried to get the racetrack reopened when I returned to the estate in the early nineties," Gordon-Lennox told me. "It was quite a challenge. The local authorities weren't keen on the plan, and it became obvious that it wasn't going to happen. We were curious to find out what we could achieve and what that might look like. I had the idea of using the roads in front of the house, because they couldn't stop me doing that. The local authorities agreed it would be OK. The first year was very exciting."[11]

On the weekend of June 19–20, 1993, the first race meeting of the Goodwood Festival of Speed took place. The duke remembers waking up the morning of the first day, looking out his bathroom window, and watching as thousands of people descended on the property. He was expecting around three thousand people; instead, twenty-five thousand showed up. "We had nowhere to put them, and it was chaotic, but it was an amazing feeling," he said. From that day, the 1.1-mile hill climb course has hosted the annual Goodwood Festival of Speed, which has quickly become one of the premier historic motor-racing showcases.

On the back of this success, Gordon-Lennox next focused on returning racing to the circuit. "As we worked with that for a few years," he said, "we were curious to think about what could happen if we received planning permission for the racetrack. My grandfather closed it in 1966; it was used a bit for testing after that. But no one did anything with it, and we were left with a completely original 1950s racetrack. We had this completely unique venue, so the idea was 'What if we let run cars run on it from the period?' That would make it easier to get past the governing body as well. It would be great if everyone joined in, in the whole period look and feel of it, and then, I think I can remember the meeting where I said, 'Well, let's get everyone to dress up as well.'"[12]

Goodwood Revival was launched in 1998 after a meticulous restoration of the old race circuit. Since that time, nostalgia enthusiasts have flocked to Goodwood for a chance to look at historic vehicles from 1948 to 1966, taking part in the event by dressing up in vintage clothes. It is a magical step back in time without the need for a time machine. You know you are somewhere very special from the moment you walk through the gate of the estate. The Goodwood Festival of Speed and the Goodwood Revival, celebrating the pioneers of motoring and motorsport, are now the highlights of the racing season, among the largest car gatherings in the world. The event also saved the estate, and it is now self-sustaining, which was the original goal of the effort.

Where will Gordon-Lennox's purposeful curiosity take him next? "Our biggest area of curiosity is the rest of the world," he said. "How can we take the brand around the world and become known internationally?" He's working on it with a concerted social media effort and a dedicated content team. No doubt his persistence, passion, and continued curiosity will make his endeavor a success.

Curiosity has fueled your research efforts and preparation. The dress rehearsal is over; you are ready to launch! Like the Duke of Richmond, we can leap into the unknown. This is the moment to turn something that originally seemed somewhat (or totally) ridiculous into a reality—something that is possible and likely. Let's examine some of the challenges that may stand in our way of taking the leap. Purposefully curious people have shown that what excites them most is going for it despite all the potential challenges and the moments of doubt.

> *We need to set boundaries to allow our curiosity to stay focused on what matters most. Otherwise, we can end up distracted, overwhelmed by the risk and uncertainty of the journey, or even burned out.*

WHY IS IT SO HARD TO MOVE FORWARD?

At some point, you will have enough information and resources to launch your journey. Reaching the top of the mountain or solving a mystery requires a capacity to act—but obstacles to moving forward can get in the way. Three common obstacles can block us from acting: a lack of confidence, the tendency to extend the research and preparation phase beyond what is necessary, and a journey that is disillusioning.

The first obstacle, a lack of confidence, stems from our uncertainty about the project, its perceived enormity, and vagueness around the journey. Despite our research and preparation, the vastness of the task can still feel overwhelming. Raphaël Domjan, the eco-explorer who completed the first solar circumnavigation in the world and is now working on the first solar aircraft to fly to the stratosphere, says his curiosity journey was uncertain, enormous, and unpredictable, but he had to push through. "There is always a risk," Domjan said. "[The journey] with *PlanetSolar* was long—and therefore more unpredictable than a shorter trip."[13] Sometimes, projects can get scrapped because the goals we set are just too big, too vague, and impossible to stick to in the long term. Some people mentioned how easy it is to run down the wrong rabbit hole and get tied up in something that is going in the wrong direction.

This last observation leads me to the second reason for getting stuck: elongating or getting mired in the research or preparation phase. Sometimes we become stuck in these preliminary processes, afraid to finish. We grow curious about our new shiny object, research it, and find relevant and wonderful material. But once we get close to finishing the work, we may freeze. The plague of unfinished PhD dissertations is a good analogy for why we tend to leave big projects incomplete. In some academic disciplines, as many as 75 percent of doctoral students fail to complete their dissertation, and the reasons include fear of failure and perfectionism.[14]

The third obstacle is that, sometimes, the journey is not as exciting as we thought it would be. Many of the people I talked with told me that their curiosity journeys were about getting their hands dirty and making things happen, but the venture also involved long hours of tedious errands and necessary but dull tasks. George Kourounis explained that what people see on television shows or in photos about expeditions are dramatic moments that show the highlights, excitement, danger, and grandeur of a situation. But there are also big chunks of time when he and his team deal with boring yet crucial parts of the expedition. "Here's a picture of me standing in front of a bunch of lava, or here's me bracing against the wind in a hurricane," Kourounis explained.[15] "But 99 percent of the time, we're just trying to get from point A to point B, organizing logistics, and dealing with translators." None of that makes for must-see TV.

YOU CAN'T LEARN TO CYCLE BY READING A BOOK: FIVE WAYS TO MAKE THE JOURNEY WORK

Your moment of truth has arrived. Now is the time to go down the rabbit hole in search of your Wonderland. Remember that the journey is about progress, not perfection. What follows are five steps to help you get and stay on your launch.

Step 1: Set Boundaries

We need to set boundaries to focus our curiosity on what matters the most. Otherwise, we can end up distracted, overwhelmed from the risk and uncertainty of the journey, or even burned out. Graphcore CEO and cofounder Nigel Toon told me that "it comes down to having the expertise to constrain the problem so that you're not trying to do something that's too big."[16] Boundaries define the battlefield. Overabundance, whether it's an excess of time, wealth, or information, stifles purposeful curiosity.

A few effective strategies can help us create boundaries that push our curiosity journeys further. First, *prioritize*. Focus on the things that really matter. Raviv Drucker, an Israeli journalist, political commentator, and investigative reporter, helped expose several high-profile political scandals that triggered police investigations. During our conversation, Drucker highlighted how prioritizing helps him make progress during his investigations. "I write down action items that I need to complete, including people who I need to speak with, who can collaborate or confirm some part of a story; research I need to do, including anything related that has already been published; check for previous lawsuits related to the topic or subjects of the story; checking the credibility of my sources, and so on."[17] Checklists can be incredibly helpful. For some, this kind of list making is a daily routine. If you go down this route, be as specific as you can about what you need to achieve that day.

Second, *set strict deadlines*. Martin Frost, the previously discussed cofounder of CMR Surgical, noted that short timelines helped him and his team get the product to prototypes quickly. "The timelines that we give ourselves to operate on are very short indeed," he said.[18] Often, just the right amount of deadline pressure can help you work at optimum effectiveness. Zowie Broach of London's Royal College of Art and the design label Boudicca, says that the strict seasonal deadlines prominent in the fashion industry helped her develop an ability to absorb more quickly what needs to be done because she had no other choice if she was going to meet the demands of the market.[19]

Step 2: Take Small Steps to Build a Rhythm

Setting boundaries can help break down your journey into manageable steps, an important way to maintain forward momentum. Take one small and specific step at a time to form a rhythm to your work and to ensure continuous action. In sports training, this technique is called making marginal gains, or accumulating manageable tweaks and improvements every day. Over time, these tweaks add up to a substantial competitive edge.[20] Harness the power of small wins, and celebrate them. "In Antarctica," said Ben Saunders, "we would walk for ninety minutes at a time, and then we'd stop, we'd eat and drink, so the day had these very definite milestones, which was useful mentally when things were really tough. We could say, 'Whatever happens, in an hour and a half, we're going to have a break.'"[21]

Luckily, we don't have to be an astronaut or a world-class athlete to make marginal gains. Just think about your vision (what you want to achieve in the long term) to be motivated, but focus on forming a daily rhythm. Animator Daisy Jacobs explained the importance of discipline and focused work in her own curiosity journeys: "When I painted *The Bigger Picture*," she said, "I would go in from a certain time to a certain time, and between that time, I would work very creatively and I would not be sluggish or take tea breaks. I would work incredibly hard and really focus, and then I would stop and I would go home. I would relax, I would go to sleep, and then I would come back and do it again. I did that regimen for seven months, and then I did that again on the next one for ten months. It was, begin, work, stop, go home, relax, sleep, get back up, and repeat. It was incredibly regimented, but within that routine, I was alert and creatively engaged."[22]

Creating such a routine in advance gives you a sense of control. It may take you some time to reach your destination. Don't worry about the time. All you've got to do is worry about today, and tomorrow, and the next day, and you will see progress.

> Harness the power of small
> wins, and celebrate them.

Step 3: Cut Down the Intermediaries
and Other Barriers to Experience

The best way to make progress is to experience the world through your own (or your team's) eyes. Consciously cut down on intermediaries. Don Wilson, founder and CEO of Chicago-based DRW, one of the most successful trading firms in the world, told me how much he loved the immediate feedback loop after building his trading models.[23] He was curious to see whether they would work. When Wilson started his career in the financial industry, he decided that he wanted to trade on the floor, because that was the most immediate feedback loop that traders could get. "Obviously," he said, "I could have worked for a bank in a trading department. But I thought, 'If I go down into the trading pit, there's no intermediary, I'm right there. You can see how the prices are moving, you can build models, you can experiment and then find out immediately what works and what doesn't. You don't need anybody to approve your model, you just do it.' I'd stand in the pit during the day and then I'd go home at night, and I would write code on my computer and build models and think about how the market behaved."[24] He could not have done that late-night analyses and learning had he sent an emissary to the trading floor.

Firsthand experience is best. Get up close and personal. Seek to experience situations as closely as possible. Ever since I was a child, I have loved music. I vividly remember buying my first vinyl record.

Then, as technology progressed, I moved on to cassette tapes and then to CDs. Today, I use a variety of streaming services, and I love the convenience and the range of songs that I have access to. At the same time, I feel detached from it. My mind is unable to remember all the music I like because of the limited engagement and interaction I have with digital formats. I do not face this problem when I have something physical in front of me. I still own a modest collection of vinyl records, and I always forget about time and place when I look at the jacket artwork, the inner sleeve, and the vinyl. The tactility of the records, reading the lyric sheets, offers a physical engagement that I find seductive. My interest gets piqued while at the same time I remember more about the artists and their songs.

We need to step outside our own narrow perspective and look up; we need to be present, speak to strangers, and push ourselves out of our comfort zone. Broach highlights the value of being physically curious: "When I started the fashion label Boudicca, there was no internet. You had to go to libraries, you had to have conversations with friends, who could help open up doors of thought and introductions to people and things. Doing the groundwork for the line wasn't about putting a word into a search engine and seeing a thousand images appear."[25]

Lionel Barber, the journalist and editor discussed earlier in the book, tries to visit at least two or three countries a year and immerses himself in their respective cultures.[26] He is intrigued to see how people live in other countries. Polar explorers like Felicity Aston want to see other environments for themselves. "If I'm curious about what does Franz Josef Land [a Russian archipelago in the Arctic Ocean] look like," she says, "I can type it into the internet, and I can see wonderful pictures. And now, increasingly, you can experience more immersive media. But I still want to see it for myself."[27]

Step 4: Create Your Own Tools

The newness of your journey might require tools that don't exist off the shelf. Don't feel limited by the tools you can find only in the market. Instead, focus on tinkering and developing tools that are essential to reaching your goals. You may have to create the parachutes as you jump off the plane. As described earlier, investigative journalist Håkon Høydal worked with the IT expert Einar Stangvik, who developed an analytical methodology to filter a vast amount of data to find the online usernames and IP and email addresses of the people who were operating and visiting the world's largest child-abuse site.[28] From this information, they then used online, open-source investigative techniques to uncover who these people really were.[29] The team's goal was to obtain their telephone numbers so that Høydal and Stangvik could contact them. "There was a huge technical effort to do that," Høydal recalled. "To go from the online data and to bring them out in the real world took months."[30]

The scientists and engineers at D-Wave, the leading manufacturer of quantum computers, frequently create their own tools to push boundaries in this space. Because they are involved in hundreds of projects, having their own machine shop inside the company enables them to build prototype parts and tools. Former CEO Vern Brownell said that the team "actually built sophisticated superconducting electronic chips. Then, on the software side, there were many tools and algorithms they had to develop, along with design, modeling, and simulation tools."[31]

Step 5: Take Corrective Actions

You're not likely to get everything right the first time. Don't worry. You will probably go down several paths that will not turn out to be right, but in doing so, you will learn, move forward, and ask better questions next time. Take corrective actions, and get on with it. Adopt two simple but critical strategies to help in this process: actively seek guidance and answers from other people, and identify patterns in light of the emerging information that you collect and analyze.

Curiosity journeys are about getting out of our comfort zone and actively listening to those who see things differently. Gordon-Lennox told me that he loves seeing how the people attending the Goodwood events respond to a range of new experiences: "I'm less curious about the numbers of people than I am in seeing how people respond to particular experiences, and how they respond to certain types of behavior."[32] Feedback is of the essence. When you receive feedback from people who see things differently and question your rightness, look at it as an opportunity to make progress. Brownell said, "One of the advantages that we have over other quantum computing efforts is that we have real customers who offer guidance. They say we would like this feature or that, and that information allows us to prioritize what we're doing. We have folks at Google, a client, in a deep dialogue. Our customers are early adopters in quantum computing and quite sophisticated, so their feedback has value."[33]

John Wiley, who led the redesign of Google Search and cofounded Google's augmented reality and VR efforts, told me that the best actors and performers do a lot of listening, and not just with their ears: "They're paying attention to what's happening around them, picking up on subtle cues, and responding to them. That's what makes a performance authentic, it resonates with an audience. I think we have to do that as technologists when we're building products, which is, be careful listeners. This means paying attention to what people are doing, how they're using products, how they're using the technology. The limitations of that technology, the challenges that they're having of the environment—it's paying careful attention to those things that helps us figure out which path to follow."[34]

When you receive feedback from people who see things differently and question your rightness, look at it as an opportunity to make progress.

Developing expertise is all about pattern recognition. Hone your discovery capabilities by looking for and recognizing patterns. Kourounis told me how terrified he felt the moment when he felt his weight on the rope and was about to dangle over a crater of fire: "But, here's the way I look at it: It's all about pattern recognition. I can look at the sky during a severe thunderstorm, and I can tell you if it's likely to produce a tornado soon. It comes down to pattern recognition, and seeing what's going on around you, and having situational awareness."[35]

Zar Amrolia studied physics at Imperial College London before earning his doctorate in mathematics from the University of Oxford. "I started off in finance, and J.P. Morgan hired me because of my math background. It was the beginning of the derivatives era in the late 1980s, and it was like learning a whole different language."[36] Eventually, he became the cohead of fixed income, currencies, and commodities at Deutsche Bank AG before leaving in 2015 to start (with Alexander Gerko, a science fiction fan with a PhD in mathematics from Moscow State University) XTX Markets, as he became increasingly curious about the algorithmic trading world. XTX Markets doesn't employ any human traders. Computers using machine learning trade assets electronically on exchanges around the world. The company's algorithms automatically learn and improve from experience without being explicitly reprogrammed.

Digesting all the information of the day piques Amrolia's interest and helps him recognize patterns. He explained: "What tends to happen is, I go home, the information percolating in my brain. I relax, go to bed, and wake up the next day able to put two and two together, and then I can fire off an email and say, 'Okay, look, guys, this is what we should be doing.'"[37]

You can improve your ability to recognize patterns by retreating to a private space and getting away from everything. Declutter your mind by disconnecting and distancing yourself—when you walk away from the problem, the aha moments often happen and solutions flow. It is not only about decompressing from the journey, Barber told me. "You can't be constantly stimulated," he said. "You need to find time to reflect. When I'm on an airplane, I'm not always reading; I just think about things. I cycle a lot, so I think about things on the bike."[38] It is also about reflection. "At the end of a trip," he noted, "I always write something down, and that requires reflection. I write a diary entry or take simple notes." When you return to your project and teams, you will have more energy and greater clarity of thinking.

Taking the leap into the unknown is akin to love. It is hard to explain; we endure pain for the joy that comes with discovering more about our shiny object. Once you have a new project and are done with planning, go out and do it. Step out of your comfort zone, chart new territory, and savor the progress you make.

– THE TAKEAWAYS –

- Understand the three things that prevent you from moving ahead: (1) uncertainty and lack of confidence, (2) unnecessarily long preparation, and (3) concern that the work involved will be tedious and unpleasant.

- Use a five-step strategy to make the curiosity journey work:
  1. Set boundaries.
  2. Take small steps to build a rhythm.
  3. Cut down the intermediaries so that you experience the world through your own (or your team's) eyes. Get up close and personal to foster direct experiences with all your senses. Virtual replicas can never replace the real thing.
  4. Create your own tools when necessary.
  5. Take corrective actions by following two simple but critical strategies: actively seek guidance and answers from other people, and identify patterns based on emerging information.

EIGHT

Develop Resilience in the Face of Adversity

> Every adversity has the seed of an equivalent or greater benefit.
> —NAPOLEON HILL, SUCCESS THROUGH A POSITIVE MENTAL ATTITUDE

AS DESCRIBED EARLIER IN THE BOOK, HAZEL FORSYTH, SENIOR CURATOR of the Museum of London's Medieval and Post-Medieval Collections, was asked to write a book on the Great Fire of London to accompany an exhibition scheduled to run in a year's time.[1] Receiving the assignment in the autumn of 2015, Forsyth had ten months to research the topic, find an interesting angle, and complete a book manuscript while performing her full-time job as a senior curator. She discovered that up to this point, most of what had been written about the fire focused on the reconstruction of the city. Forsyth was more interested in the people who had survived the fire and what became of them. The blaze had started on September 2, 1666, and lasted for four days.[2] It devastated the city but forced

London into a period of rebirth. What impact did the fire have on the population? How did Londoners, particularly women, survive? Those were the kinds of questions that guided Forsyth as she immersed herself in research.[3] She focused on the period from 1660 to 1675. Forsyth chose the first date to gain a sense of Londoners' lives before the fire; the second date coincides with the final phase of reconstruction, when most people had gotten their businesses back up and running.[4]

Having a deadline forced Forsyth to quickly draw up a list of source material to explore. Wasting little time, she checked all surviving documentation from London's civic and corporate institutions. She sorted through boxes of archives, tracing the journey through letters, diaries, and court documents. She ran every conceivable search that she could think of on the London Metropolitan Archives database and the UK government's National Archives. The experience was overwhelming, but gradually she started making sense of what she was finding.

Many times, Forsyth would come across references that seemed promising but that, once pursued, didn't prove helpful. It was disappointing. "Sometimes you can follow the thread and see [something of value], and sometimes you come to a dead end, and you have to retrack," she told me. "Those not engaged in research often think that it must be possible to find the evidence. But of course, it is not always possible. It can be dispiriting, and you wonder whether you're barking up the wrong tree because what you hope survives isn't there, so you have to take a different route, a different angle."

Despite feeling beaten up by the work, Forsyth tried to focus on the positive. Even hitting a research wall is progress of sorts, what she calls negative evidence, because the absence of material can be valuable information. "People that don't do primary research perhaps don't appreciate the labor involved," she said. "Sometimes you must force yourself to read and read and read even if, at the end of each day, you don't find a single thing. But you have to keep going in the hope that suddenly you'll turn a page and there will be something that you can use. Sometimes the lack of evidence—negative evidence—is almost as important as the evidence itself."

Forsyth's resilience helped her keep trying. "I think you have to have at least some structure to work with, and it may be that you have to modify that structure according to things that you find," she explained. She continued to go through documents until she found one that turned out to be a register of sheds. The document had been compiled by the Corporation of London (the governing body of the City of London) for a roughly seven-year period after the fire. It listed about 130 people, their occupations, the rental values, and where the sheds were located.[5] When Forsyth found this register, her heart palpitated and her eyes widened. After the fire, this rather ramshackle structural solution was a carefully-thought-through scheme that generated money for the corporation but, importantly, provided relatively secure lodgings for the occupants.[6] The result of her work, the fascinating book *Butcher, Baker, Candlestick Maker*, describes how citizens, institutions, and traders—including apothecaries, bakers, upholsterers, and watchmakers—rebuilt their lives and restored London's prosperity after the Great Fire.[7]

> *Every time we reach key milestones in our curiosity journeys and come closer to our destination, we feed our brain with the joy of achievement.*

WHAT DOESN'T KILL YOU . . . MAKES YOU MORE CURIOUS

Curiosity journeys like the one Forsyth took are emotional roller coasters. The highs are marked by our achieving what we set out to do. They are exhilarating. The lows, when our efforts don't seem to be paying off, are frustrating and defeating. We build perseverance by imagining what we can do. Every time we reach key milestones in our curiosity journeys and come closer to our destination, we feed our brain with the joy of achievement. This was certainly the case for Hazel Forsyth. The ability to push through frustrations and perceived impasses increases our belief in our ability to handle challenging situations and can produce a rush of the neurotransmitter dopamine to our brains; this chemical propels us to carry on, to do more. Like Forsyth, we should approach setbacks with determination and vigor rather than giving in to the temptation to retreat and give up.

The road to long-term success is never a straight line. We can feel tempted to throw in the towel when faced with setbacks. Hitting an obstacle can often make us feel stuck. We may even panic. The feeling that we cannot control everything can destabilize us, can leave us feeling powerless, and can block our curiosity. Amid adversity, defeatist thoughts such as "I don't want to do this project anymore," "I am sick of the work," or "I can't do it" are inevitable.

What makes some people pursue the unknown with zeal despite setbacks while others give up when the going gets tough? Resilience, a trait that we are not born with, involves the interplay between our natural dispositions and external experiences. Even as children, we can learn the skills that make us more resilient, more willing to tough it out as we maneuver demanding situations. It can be fostered with practice and patience.[8] Purposeful curiosity allows us to get back on track quickly and learn from our mistakes.

What doesn't kill you makes you more curious: The more we put ourselves in situations or environments that are new to us and that challenge us, the more we develop skills and coping mechanisms to face those challenges. "Choose curiosity, don't surrender," our inner voice tells us. If we adopt this approach, something interesting will start happening: our curiosity will deepen; we will become more interested in finding out why things don't work.

As we move along the path from elaborate preparations to practicing to the journey itself, uncertainty is bound to increase. As the old proverb says, "We plan, God laughs." But when something goes wrong, we seldom find the wherewithal to join in the laughter. Some things will always be unpredictable. We'll face surprises, questions with no solid answers, and variables outside our control during our curiosity endeavors. We will feel powerless. So, we must become comfortable with the idea that we will fail numerous times. We have to learn from our failures and pick ourselves up and carry on.

There is much we can do to help ourselves and our teams navigate the darkest days of our curiosity journeys. Five actionable approaches help build our resilience muscle so that we emerge victorious on the other side of adversity:

- Quickly reconnect to your purpose.
- Change your narrative.
- Create a strong support network.
- Put positive emotions to work.
- Crack each setback like a detective.

QUICKLY RECONNECT TO YOUR PURPOSE

Kazuhide Sekiyama was a high school student when he met his future mentor, Masaru Tomita, the founder of the Institute for

Advanced Biosciences of Keio University in Japan. Professor Tomita visited Sekiyama's school to talk about his research and present Keio University programs to prospective students.[9] During the presentation, Tomita argued that developments in computer science and biotechnology would help us solve complex problems like sustainability and climate change.[10] Sekiyama's curiosity was immediately stirred, and after graduating from high school, he enrolled at Keio University. During the final year of his undergraduate degree, he started researching different areas, including protein material. Sekiyama wanted to focus on a curiosity project that no one had yet achieved, one that could have a significant impact on society. Finding a project that fit these criteria became his goal. "I can't just innovate for innovation's sake," he told me. "There has to be an underlying motivation that's strong, not just in terms of what kind of technology you want to achieve but why you are trying to create some new technology. And if that motivation is there, then you study what you need to study to accomplish that."

Three years later, he founded Spiber, a biomaterials company based in Japan. Spiber re-created the DNA designs of spiders to produce an artificial material that does not depend on petroleum the way that other synthetic fibers such as polyester and nylon do.[11] Spiber's proprietary Brewed Protein material is a bio-based, biodegradable, and animal-free synthetic protein platform.[12] It can replace cashmere, wool, fur, leather, silk, and other animal or petroleum-based materials, using fewer natural resources.[13] By building up the infrastructure needed to master the production of these materials on an industrial level, Spiber is striving to bring about a more sustainable society.[14]

Sekiyama said that to carry on and create breakthroughs while experiencing setbacks, "you have to have a strong core that allows you to persist through lots of hardships."[15] For Sekiyama and his cofounders, knowing the human impact of what they are pursuing keeps them going. Their purpose sustains them, and they remind themselves of it often. Their purpose not only channels their curiosity but also helps them maintain perspective when they most need it. The faster we reconnect to our purpose, the faster we can pick ourselves up and continue problem-solving.

> *If we want to make progress on our curiosity journeys, we must see the positive in every negative—the brighter side in almost any situation.*

CHANGE YOUR NARRATIVE

Remember the last time you struggled with adversity in your life? Now take a deep breath and try to recall what you did. Did you pick apart every mistake that led you into that situation? Did you turn the difficulty into an opportunity to blame yourself for every setback life had thrown at you? Did you hear a little voice pushing you to quit? If you answered yes to these questions, you are likely to see a setback as a disaster.

If we want to make progress on our curiosity journeys, we must see the positive in every negative—the brighter side in almost any situation. We must see the setback as an opportunity to intentionally explore rather than as a disaster to impulsively react to. Raviv Drucker, the Israeli investigative journalist previously discussed, told me that his curiosity is centered around important stories that typically don't see the light of the press.[16] He is attracted to investigating stories that people don't speak about (e.g., high-profile scandals in politics, sexual harassment cases, and corporate fraud). Drucker is fascinated by topics that will make "the listener or the viewer or the reader say, 'Oh my god, I didn't know that.'" Because of the complexity and seriousness of these cases, Drucker says he "hits the wall so many times." Insufficient evidence or dead ends with people unwilling to talk may take him nowhere or to nowhere new. By not getting blocked by every wall that he hits and by instead perceiving these hurdles as opportunities to further explore, Drucker, like a police investigator, continues going through pages of evidence, talking to more sources, fact-checking, and being skeptical about or questioning many things to solve a case.

"If I hit a wall, I know that there is a story I'm fascinated with, which helps me treat the story as an almost egoistic challenge. I need to prove it," he said. "Maybe it will go this direction, this fact will fall, other facts will prove the truth," he said. When faced with uncertainty, we must ask ourselves: "How do I turn this setback into an opportunity to further explore?" This framing will help us continue our work.

Chen Reiss, the Israeli operatic soprano we met earlier in the book, began piano studies at the age of five, ballet at the age of seven, and voice lessons at fourteen.[17] She decided to focus on vocal studies when she was sixteen.[18] Reiss has established a strongly acclaimed and distinctive career, performing leading parts at the Vienna State Opera, the Royal Opera House in Covent Garden, and the Bavarian State Opera. Reiss told me that she had many disappointments when she was starting her career. She endured arduous auditions that never resulted in her getting a part in an opera. Many of her opera singer friends gave up, she told me. She persisted. "It's a journey of trusting yourself and believing in your ability even when it seems no one else does," she told me. Success will come if you continue to believe you can do it, practice, and continue to show up. In Reiss's case, this approach meant continuing to audition, believing that she would eventually get a part.

By believing in ourselves, we develop an inner dialogue that can continually feed us with images, thoughts, and beliefs of success. When we change the narrative in our heads ("I am going to learn from this; I will gain from this setback"), we tend to see the brighter side of almost any situation. Telling ourselves a better story rather than focusing on the worst-case scenario is a powerful tool in our arsenal for surviving any challenge, crisis, or other adversity that we encounter in our curiosity journeys.

When we change the narrative, we will feel less negative and will free our minds up to find solutions to our problems. Internally driven, we need to find that place within us—a place that grounds and comforts us. By writing down a setback that we recently experienced and exploring new opportunities, different options, or new ways to approach things because of this setback, we move one step closer to our success. We must think of setbacks as stepping stones in our curiosity journey. It can't all be sunshine and gloriousness; there have to be darker days for us to appreciate the better days.

> *By believing in ourselves, we develop an inner dialogue that can continually feed us with images, thoughts, and beliefs of success.*

CREATE A STRONG SUPPORT NETWORK

None of us can go at it alone. We can develop resilience more easily when we surround ourselves with people who understand the adversity we face and cheer us on when needed. Establishing and nurturing a supportive social network can boost our emotional strength during times of stress. Other people's determination can help us carry on when we think of giving up. "So, to be able to have a colleague who said, 'No, no, no, let's stick to this,' is crucial," Håkon Høydal said.[19] He told me that the support he received from his editors was hugely important because they allowed him and his partner to work on the online child-abuse project for a long time. His editors believed in the importance of the work and gave him the resources and time to pursue it.

If you do not have an in-person network of supportive friends, family members, or colleagues, you can create one by seeking out those who have endured adversity. Start by going online. Search purposefully for people who have made it. For instance, you might look for presenters in conferences or talks in the area of your interest and reach out to them. Websites and social media platforms such as Facebook, Meetup, Nextdoor, LinkedIn, and Instagram offer opportunities to find local events of interest. Organized classes can be a wonderful way to find like-minded people who have been successful in their journeys. You can search online for continuing education courses at local colleges or universities, where you will meet professors and classmates who may be able to offer useful advice and curiosity comradery.

According to a 2016 behavioral study published in *Neuron*, when we interact with someone who performs well, our estimates of our own abilities improve.[20] If we associate with people who have pushed through roadblocks on journeys similar to our own, not only will we start adopting the mindset that helps us make progress but we'll also pick up the activities that will enable us to get there. Modeling the behavior and habits of people who have attained their curiosity journeys helps us push through.

PUT POSITIVE EMOTIONS TO WORK

Adrian Newey is widely regarded as one of the world's greatest engineers in motor-racing history. He is currently the chief technical officer of the Red Bull Racing Formula One team.[21] Newey's designs have won numerous titles and more than 150 Grand Prix. He is the only engineer to have won ten Constructors' Championships titles with three different Formula One teams.[22] After graduating from the University of Southampton in England with a first-class honors degree in aeronautics and astronautics, Newey started working for the Fittipaldi Formula One team.[23]

After his short stint at Fittipaldi, he joined the March Formula One team, where he started designing racing cars, and in 1984, he moved to the American IndyCar project.[24] Newey experienced his first successes in the United States when his car designs proved highly competitive and very quickly started winning Championship Auto Racing Teams competitions and the most prestigious event in America, the Indianapolis 500, for three consecutive years (1985, 1986, and 1987).[25] Despite all these wins, Newey decided to return to Europe because of his passion for Formula One.[26] After brief stints at different Formula One teams, such as FORCE and March, he joined the Williams team, where in collaboration with Patrick Head (the cofounder and technical director of Williams), he brought home five Constructors' titles between 1992 and 1997.[27] When he left Williams for McLaren (another prestigious Formula One team), it didn't take him long to deliver. He took McLaren to the Constructors' title in 1998. After all the success at Williams and McLaren, Newey faced a fresh challenge when he joined Red Bull Racing. For this young team without pedigree, winning championships was a difficult task.[28] Newey's revolutionary car designs won Red Bull Racing four Constructors' Championship titles from 2010 to 2013.[29] The Red Bull team's win on August 24, 2014, marked Newey's 150th Grand Prix victory in Formula One.[30]

In the fiercely competitive world of racing, where second-best is never acceptable, nasty surprises are not unheard-of, Newey told me.[31] New car designs are thoroughly researched, and they look great in the lab. Yet when they hit the track, they don't perform as well as expected. Resilience in such situations is not an optional add-on but a mandatory skill for success. Newey's solution for going back to the drawing board is to depersonalize the problem and focus on "making sure that everybody continues to treat it as an engineering problem, [to think] that there is a reason why it's not working. It's just we don't understand it yet, so we've got to try to put all the theories forward."

Gershon Tenenbaum, professor of sport and exercise psychology at Florida State University, is an expert in coping with physical effort experiences. "When pressure increases, negative feelings like anxiety affect our attention, making it narrow," he told me.[32] We must be coolheaded at times of crisis. All the problems that we experience in our curiosity journey are not about us; they are simply things that we must deal with. This approach makes us less emotional, which in turn gives us more clarity of response. "Attention to our negative feelings doesn't allow us to attend to all the important cues in the environment, and therefore our decision-making is limited," Tenenbaum explained. By learning to relax, taking a break from current setbacks, and engaging in a pleasant activity or reflecting on past enjoyable experiences, we can cultivate positive emotions. In return, these emotions can help us feel calm, focused, and committed, so that we can continue to dig into the reasons for the setback or failures.

CRACK EACH SETBACK LIKE A DETECTIVE

We should perceive setbacks on our curiosity journeys as crossword puzzles, things that engage our brains rather than our emotions. We should force ourselves to dig deeper into the problems and understand why the project didn't work. Four steps can help us crack each setback like a detective:

1. Formulate a plan to give yourself a path forward.
2. Break down the setback into its components.

3. Take time to process the evidence.
4. Shift to a new direction when you hit a dead end.

1. Formulate a Plan to Give Yourself a Path Forward

Establish the perimeter of the setback. Write down in detail how you will control the impact of the setback and get yourself back on track. What can you do to get moving again? According to a study by Shevaun Neupert, a psychology professor, and her team at North Carolina State University, it's essential to keep making plans.[33] Planning fosters a positive mindset and acts as a shield against feeling incapacitated by stress.[34] It also guards us from procrastination.[35] We need to figure out what went wrong and focus on making a plan to deal with the setback.

A proven strategy that helps move us through setbacks and even solve them is journaling or writing. Most of the time we solve problems using an analytical perspective, but sometimes we can find better answers using our intuition and feelings. Freeform journaling encourages us to look to our feelings. It helps unlock our creative side and allows for unexpected solutions to difficult problems. Numerous academic studies have shown the benefits of keeping a journal. Philip Ullrich and Susan Lutgendorf, professors of psychology at University of Iowa, for instance, found that doing so helps us organize and make sense of events, giving us a way of putting setbacks in perspective and seeing them as a small tree in the forest of our lives.[36] Krista Fritson, psychology professor at the University of Nebraska at Kearney, also found that students who keep journals exhibit increasing self-efficacy and have a healthy sense of control over their lives.[37] Moreover, Joshua Smyth, professor of behavioral health and medicine at Pennsylvania State University, and his team discovered that journaling can reduce mental distress and enhance psychological, interpersonal, and physical well-being among older adults with significant anxiety.[38]

═══ KEEP A SETBACK DIARY ═══

We all like to forget about the obstacles that we face, but we should be open to learning from these experiences. Keep a diary where you record the roadblocks that you faced in your curiosity journeys, how you overcame them, and what you learned from them.

2. Break Down the Setback into Its Components

To recover from a problem (rather than be a victim of it), we must pause to break down the setback into its smaller components to unpack the problem. Tenenbaum, who has studied and worked with numerous professional athletes, highlighted the importance of delving deeper into the setback and collecting evidence to figure out what is going wrong. When athletes are not performing well, they have to understand what is not working. "Find out from the athlete what the reason is. It can be bad relations with the family, it can be bad relations with a spouse, it can be something that we don't know," Tenenbaum told me.[39]

3. Take Time to Process the Evidence

If you've pursued a curiosity project for a couple of weeks without reaching a desired milestone, it is normal to want to stop and try another direction. Resist the urge to do this, and stay on your current route long enough to get some answers on what's not working.

Hitting a wall is often more valuable than the experiments that work from the get-go. Instead of leaving us feeling stuck and powerless, hurdles can empower our excitement and heighten our curiosity—if we ask *why*. Rocket Lab founder Peter Beck noted that "when things fail, it forces you to dig much deeper into 'Well, hang on a minute—I expected that to work and it didn't. Now I need to really understand why it didn't.'"[40] Hadsell, the previously cited senior research scientist at Google DeepMind, advises those on a curiosity journey to make sure that they answer all the questions on their present path before choosing a new one. When it comes to experiments, it's not about success or failure; it's about outcome and learning.

NOT ALL SETBACKS ARE BORN EQUAL

To determine which problems to pay attention to and which to ignore, conduct a *setback reality check* to understand the effects of the obstacle that you are currently facing. Not all setbacks are of equal magnitude. Imagine yourself ten years forward, talking to your loved ones about one of the biggest setbacks that you managed to overcome. Would you talk about the one that you are currently facing? If this is not the one, then it means that this problem is not as significant as you originally thought. If it is, then you need to further understand it.

4. Shift to a New Direction when You Hit a Dead End

There is such a thing as excessive experimentation: being caught up in a cycle of testing and validating because we are not getting the results we hoped for and we don't want our assumptions to be wrong. Roger Ibbotson, academic, hedge fund manager, and pioneering analyst, told me that the preconceived notions we may have on a curiosity journey may not necessarily be correct. We can't allow our bias to stop us from finding the right answers. "You have to recognize your mistakes, expect that you're going to be wrong, and adapt," he said.[41]

After studying mathematics for his undergraduate degree, Ibbotson earned his PhD at the University of Chicago. "That was a place where a lot of big discoveries were taking place," he told me. "I was in an exciting research environment when I was working toward my PhD, and then I went on as a professor, but I also started a business. I had always wanted to see how you could apply academic ideas to practice." Ibbotson dedicated his academic life (and, later, his professional life) to investigating large data sets to discover how stocks behave. His thesis was that popularity makes a difference: that unpopular stocks are relatively undervalued while popular stocks are at least fully valued.[42] To test his thesis, Ibbotson ran many tests, some of which led to dead ends. But he didn't quit; he persevered by shifting into new directions. "I guess it's that happy medium between not quitting every time you fail at something and recognizing when you must shift," he said.

Like Ibbotson, we shouldn't get stuck on any one path. We must become comfortable with knowing that some of our efforts will lead to dead ends. In my career as an academic, I have experienced setbacks like this several times. When I hit a snag, my focus has always been on how to move forward. I once conducted a study on the management of succession in family businesses in Greece. I reviewed existing academic literature on succession in family firms, developed questions to ask family members, and booked my trip to Athens to collect data. I sought to interview different generations running family firms (children, parents, and, sometimes, grandparents). I reached out to several family businesses, some of which agreed to participate.

During the initial interview with the first family business, I noticed when I explained that my research project was about how these family businesses would manage succession, the parent owners became defensive and hesitant to share their plans. I thought their attitude might be a fluke, but the next interview with another parent owner played out in the same way.

Something was holding these families back from talking about succession. I have a friend who works in his family's business, and I explained to him what had happened in the interviews. His response was eye-opening. Apparently, parents in family firms in Greece don't like the word *succession* because they associate it with their own death. They consider succession a taboo and, hence, don't want to talk about it. I took his advice on board and replaced the word *succession* with *long-term planning* in subsequent interviews. Shifting to this new direction paid off. Parents in family firms were happy to talk about long-term planning and shared their thoughts about it—they were happy to talk about succession as long as we didn't use that term.

> *By learning to relax, taking a break from current setbacks, and engaging in a pleasant activity or reflecting on past enjoyable experiences, we can cultivate positive emotions.*

As a mentor or an adviser to several start-ups, I have seen more than one team fail to find its first customer or secure external funding because it focused on finding answers that didn't exist instead of pivoting when necessary. A start-up I once mentored raised millions of dollars from investors, which it spent on expanding its workforce, opening offices around the world, and developing an aggressive advertising campaign. Yet all these noteworthy investments did not increase revenues. Why? It could have been that the product lacked a robust or sustainable market, the target audience was not moved by the company's message, the market was unwilling to pay the asking price, or the industry that the start-up operated in was saturated. In this case, the problem was that the product wasn't clearly differentiated from its direct competitors. As a result, despite all the start-up's investments, the market saw no value in giving the product a try.

Pivoting is a humbling process. It's a matter of swallowing our pride, understanding where our journey is heading, and deciding on a potentially drastic course of action. If our curiosity journey is radically underperforming or flat-out dead in the water, a pivot is the way to go.

WHEN IS IT TIME TO PIVOT?

The best part of curiosity is knowing when not to persevere. Answer these two questions by taking an honest, objective look. Let go of any emotions that involve your hope for results!

- Do you carry on, spending resources and time on the same path, when you are not hitting the mark?

- Are you constantly (not occasionally, which is expected) getting negative feedback about your journey regardless of the hard work and resources you put in?

If you've answered yes to both questions, you may need to pivot to a different route on your curiosity journey.

I have always enjoyed playing video games. They mirror curiosity journeys and are a useful metaphor for, and a way to practice resilience, persistence, pivoting, and problem-solving. In my early twenties, I was obsessed with *Quake*, a first-person 3D video game in which I had to find my way through the dark and scary maze-like, medieval world battling different creatures. I loved exploring new worlds, the uneasiness of finding myself in an inescapable bad dream, and, of course, the euphoria of getting out of it. If I couldn't escape and failed, I never idolized it. Failure is emotionally painful, even when you're playing a video game.

Yet at the same time, I always viewed setbacks in the game as learning opportunities to grow, develop resilience, and keep trying. They kept me sharp. Each failure was central to my enjoyment of the journey; it became a learning exercise. Every new puzzle required more training of my reflexes, further observation, and a new way of thinking. Backed up by a strong belief (or naivete) that I would improve with practice, I held myself responsible for my actions, sought to understand my downfalls (rather than criticize them), and asked myself how I could deal with setbacks. A new strange and growing bond was developing with every attempt between the game and me. I was growing my resilience muscle. Building resilience, like working out, requires dedication, focus, and a lot of sweat. Success tastes sweeter when you overcome obstacles through effort.

Curiosity journeys are about hitting blockades often, and failing. But they are also about picking ourselves up and carrying on. We shouldn't get distracted by the adrenaline rush of the unknown; we need to remain calm, mentally focused, and emotionally disciplined. We must get comfortable with being uncomfortable. In our curiosity projects, enjoyment will not be the protagonist. What will take center stage is the sensation of stretching the boundaries of what we can do, the feeling of being sore after running six miles when we have only ever run three miles before. Reflecting on past successes will be reassuring, but we must push ourselves to go where we don't want to go, focus on what doesn't work, and figure out ways to overcome these things. When setbacks hit and we feel low, we have a choice: Either we can drop even lower or even give up, or we can pick ourselves back up and remind ourselves (and our teams) of our purpose and fight for more. We should never give up or feel defeated; instead, like children who try innumerable things, fail, and try again, we must keep going and try new paths. We should be unrelenting. There is always another move.

– THE TAKEAWAYS –

There are five actionable things you can do right now to help you overcome setbacks and build your resilience muscle during your curiosity journeys:

- Reconnect to your purpose. Remind yourself what brought you here. Purpose matters. When setbacks hit us, we need to rediscover why we pursued our curiosity object in the first place. Why do we want this so badly? Who will we become once we've crossed the finish line? What will life look like when we've reached our destination?
- Change your narrative. Reframe the setback as an opportunity to intentionally explore rather than as a disaster to react to impulsively.
- Create a strong support network. Developing resilience is easier when we partner with people who understand the adversity we face and cheer us on when needed.
- Put your positive emotions to work. Negative emotions are out; positive ones are in. We should avoid panicking when we hit the wall during our curiosity journeys. Our hearts can cloud our judgment when we are in emergency mode. In-

stead, we should get more excited and interested when things don't work; we need to put our positive emotions to work.

- Crack each setback like a detective:
  - » Formulate a plan to give yourself a path forward. Establish the perimeter of the setback. Write down in detail how you will deal with the situation.
  - » Break down the setback into smaller components, and start collecting evidence to analyze these components further.
  - » Take time to process the evidence. Hitting a wall challenges us to be curious; to ask open-ended questions; to actively experiment with theories, frameworks, and tools; to explore a different angle; to gather and analyze the relevant data; and to see where this insight may take us.
  - » Shift to a new direction when you hit a dead end. Recognize when your taken path doesn't hit the mark. Pivot, and try something else.

NINE

Turn the Ending into Your New Beginning

> *When you reach the end of what you should*
> *know, you will be at the beginning of what*
> *you should sense.*
>
> —KAHLIL GIBRAN

MAE CAROL JEMISON WAS BORN ON OCTOBER 17, 1956, IN DECATUR, Alabama, and raised in Chicago.[1] Her parents encouraged her curiosity from an early age. As a child, Jemison spent hours in the school library. She was interested in all aspects of science, especially astronomy. Whatever piqued her curiosity was very likely to turn into a project. In an interview for *Stanford Today*, Jemison shared that her mother always encouraged her to do her own independent research on the topics that interested her.[2] "It's your responsibility [to look it up]," Jemison recalls her mother telling her whenever she didn't know something.[3]

Jemison wanted to study biomedical engineering, but there was no course in that field at that time.[4] As a result, at just sixteen, she enrolled in the chemical engineering program at Stanford University. After completing her studies, she continued to pursue her interest in biomedical engineering and went on to study medicine at Cornell University. She graduated with an MD degree from Weill Cornell Medical College in 1981. During her time at the medical school, Jemison visited several countries, including Kenya and Cuba, to offer medical care and to satisfy a lifelong desire to understand different cultures.

After working in various medical centers and volunteering in the Peace Corps in West Africa, she joined insurance company Cigna as a general practitioner while taking graduate engineering classes. Jemison's insatiable curiosity about what lies beyond our planet led her to her next adventure and to follow another childhood fascination: space exploration. She applied to NASA's astronaut program and was accepted in 1987. Jemison was one of fifteen candidates chosen from a pool of about two thousand.[5] She completed her training in 1988. On September 12, 1992, at thirty-six, she became the first Black woman to go into space. Jemison served as a mission specialist, serving with six other astronauts aboard the space shuttle *Endeavour*. Jemison subsequently made significant advancements in space-related science and travel and received several awards, including several honorary doctorates.

Jemison is a stellar example of how the satisfaction of our curiosity can lead to the beginning of new curiosity adventures. In March 1993, Jemison left NASA not to rest on her laurels but to found businesses, a foundation, and an international science camp (the Earth We Share). She became a college professor and an advocate for science education and health care.

Whether it is accomplishing a personal goal, such as graduating from college, or achieving a professional milestone, like getting the job you've always wanted, starting your own business, or launching a new product, you should feel grateful for everything that you have accomplished. But, like Jemison, you shouldn't let it end there. Your best performances and projects are in front of you, not behind you.

We should never lose our sense of restless curiosity, and we don't have to. We can shift gracefully from the ending of one curiosity project to the beginning of another. Curiosity can strike again when we take the time to reflect on the outcome of our curiosity projects and answer a simple but critical question: "Am I still curious enough to continue to explore this field or arena?" Our response will shape our paths, of which there are usually two: On path A, we continue to be interested in exploring new aspects of the field. And following path B, we feel that we have exhausted this area and want to explore a new one. Whatever path we will decide to take after the finish line, one thing is clear: purposeful curiosity is a train from which we never have to alight.

> *We can shift gracefully from the ending of one curiosity project to the beginning of another.*

THE DOWNSIDE OF CROSSING THE FINISH LINE

Once you've reached your destination after weeks, months, or even years of effort, commitment, and sacrifice, you may find that embarking on a new journey seems more challenging than you imagined. There are three common reasons why this shift can leave your pioneering spirit feeling stuck: (1) the anticlimax that follows the high of satisfying your curiosity, (2) the presumed difficulty of finding another exciting project, and (3) the daunting or exhausting prospect of embarking on a new journey after just finishing one.

Feeling anticlimactic after an arduous effort is the equivalent of standing on the summit of a high mountain, having accomplished a feat very few people have mastered, looking down, and thinking, "Is that it?" Despite the preparation the journey took, the high of arriving at your destination is often followed by a low. Many people who have pursued curiosity journeys, whether the undertaking was an exploration or a new business, felt profound satisfaction that they could make a positive impact on their own lives, their communities, and perhaps even the world. At the same time, many people I talked to said there was also something deflating about achieving what they had set out to do.

Endings are bittersweet. After a period of intense focus, execution, and excitement, we might anxiously wonder, "Now what? What will happen after this herculean undertaking?" There are a few explanations for this potential letdown. The first one is chemical. Every time we anticipate reaching a goal, our brains release dopamine, a neurotransmitter. Each milestone gives us a new dopamine hit, which in turn motivates us to keep doing what we do. Yet when we complete a project, that release of dopamine drops and there is a corresponding low. It is harder for us to experience joy, in a biochemical sense—and in the emotional and psychological senses.

Second, you may struggle to find a challenge as compelling as your last one. Or you may become overwhelmed with endless possibilities. Once you realize that you want to explore further, resolve a new mystery, and reach a new destination, your past success may haunt you. You might ask yourself, "How do I top that?" Alternatively, you may feel overwhelmed with all the possibilities and unable to decide which new challenge to tackle. Both kinds of thoughts can be obstacles to moving forward.

Finally, as soon as you cross your finish line, you may get better at talking yourself out of exploring new things. Designer

Michael Jager told me, "It's easy to find ten reasons why something won't work, and you think you're so clever because of it."[6] Your success may become a trap, conditioning you to stick to the familiar and making you less willing to explore novel alternatives. "When we build a business," Jager noted, "even if it's a breakthrough in the beginning, at a certain point, we start defending what we created." He meant that we protect what we created rather than innovating beyond it.

> *Settling in too early to an approach will deprive you from exciting new possibilities that you couldn't have even imagined at first.*

PERPETUAL CURIOSITY

All curiosity projects come to an end, and the aftermath is a crucial phase in our development as purposefully curious people. I am talking about the critical work that we have to do the days or weeks after reaching our destination to turn the one-off victory into a long-term winning streak. We must use this time to find new boundaries to reach for and push. For fashion designer Mary Katrantzou, it is an organic process: "An idea will lead to another idea; it's just a case of approaching that idea in a new way. It becomes the building blocks to something you will do in the future."[7]

We want to develop an emotional and intellectual state that feels as if we're on an eternal journey of perpetual curiosity. "In a strange way," British artist Gavin Turk told me, "you almost don't want to solve the mystery, because the solution would stop it from being a mystery. It would spoil it."[8] Indeed, the more knowledge we acquire, the more difficult it becomes to see the finish line of our projects, since we are always interested in exploring the next possibility. In some ways, the more we know, the less we know, because knowledge enables us to ask better, harder questions. We should be confident that we will never run out of ideas to explore, questions to answer, and riddles to solve. There is always more to learn.

How do you switch gears and refocus your energy on a new project? Reflecting on the curiosity project that you have just completed, ask yourself one crucial question: "Am I still curious about exploring this field?" Depending on your answer, there are two paths to follow. If you answer yes, you can follow path A: leverage your untapped curiosity in the field to explore new paths. If your answer is no, then follow path B: leap into a new field for your new curiosity journey. Let's look at these two paths in more detail.

Path A: Stay the Course, and Further Stretch the Boundaries of the Field

Edward Bonham Carter (the older brother of the actor Helena) studied economics and politics at the University of Manchester.[9] After graduation, he worked for several asset management companies, and in the 1990s, he joined Jupiter, a UK-based investment house that currently manages around £60 billion in assets. Interestingly, the advertising campaign that Jupiter ran for some time used curiosity as its main theme, followed by an aspirational explanation of how curiosity differentiates the company from its rivals: "It's human nature to constantly seek out more."

Bonham Carter had a successful career at Jupiter as its chief investment officer and seven years as its CEO. At the time of our conversation, he was vice chair. The key to his success? Endless questions that convert into curiosity projects. "One of the roles [as the vice chair] is to spend more time looking at long-term trends.

What are the big forces which we need to spend more time thinking about?"[10] These questions might be hard to answer if you've been in the same field for many years. Experience can make you take things for granted; with such an attitude, you could miss out on industry, cultural, and social changes that will affect your business in the long term. So how do you stay fresh in a field you are deeply familiar with?

Bonham Carter intentionally carves out time to look at open-ended questions from new angles. He contemplates different scenarios and challenges assumptions about demographics, technology, and other topics, such as poverty and climate change. "What are the challenges of populations aging in the West?" he asks. "How are we going to afford old age? What does this mean for economic growth and productivity? That's a big, big theme. The second big one is technology. Is technology going to be the answer to everything, or are there going to be some big challenges? For example, if the rate of automation increases, what are people going to do with their lives? Are we teaching the right skills for the fourth industrial age?"[11] The problems of food distribution, access to clean water and proper sanitation, and climate change are also crucial, he says. His curiosity is unbridled—and it prevents him from getting stuck in the past and from basing decisions on assumptions that are no longer relevant.

Other people I talked with offered insights into their future endeavors. Chen Reiss plans to sing in opera houses that she has not yet sung in, perform roles that she has not yet played, and make more recordings.[12] Adrian Newey talked about getting more involved with long-distance sports car racing like the Le Mans race and with smaller, more efficient cars.[13] Explorers like Felicity Aston, George Kourounis, and Ben Saunders spoke of their longing to travel to the most extreme places, documenting what they see, and eventually sharing their experiences with the world.[14] Hedge fund managers are fascinated by cryptocurrencies and other new forms of money.

In a typical hyperlink fashion, where answers inspire more questions, it's intriguing to discover the best ways to drive curiosity when you stay in the same field, even over years or decades, as Bonham Carter and others have done. Many people who are deeply engaged in their subject are confident that they will never run out of new things to discover or pursue. However, discovery does become harder in these circumstances. How do you add more items every time you check something off your bucket list? What will motivate you to learn new skills, develop new relationships, and rejuvenate your sense of purpose? How can you creatively find new and exciting mysteries to solve or projects to explore so that you will continue making an impact?

If you're ever stuck, the following tips can help rekindle your curiosity when you are staying in the same field:

Start Now

Be proactive instead of trying to revitalize the desire to continue exploring your field when the desire is lost. Every time you check something off your bucket list, add two more items at the bottom. Don Wilson, the previously mentioned founder and CEO of DRW, suggests that if you have been exploring this domain for some time, you should focus on areas that you find personally challenging and relevant in your field and that would have an impact if expanded or developed.[15] For instance, as an educator, I am excited about what education might morph into in the metaverse, or the "digital reality that combines aspects of social media, online gaming, augmented reality, VR, and cryptocurrencies to allow users to interact virtually."[16] I have started to explore how we can design a greater number of immersive learning experiences using VR. How may the metaverse help make higher education more inclusive and engaging?

Increase the Difficulty of Your Next Adventure

You can up the ante, but not so much that you end up feeling overstretched or risk failing. But don't make it so easy that you get bored. We'll want to get involved in curiosity projects where we think we are making progress because the new challenges that we face enable us to develop our skills and ingenuity.

Explore New Opportunities, and Connect Them to Past Journeys

Keep your mind actively open and on the lookout for areas that you have not explored in your field but that relate to your past journeys. Kazuhide Sekiyama, the innovator of fabric made from artificial spider silk, said that "as the CEO of Spiber, I have to find new potential opportunities and look into them, try to make connections between them so that we can explore those opportunities or start initiatives within the company to try out these new opportunities."[17] Others move beyond their field to bring new opportunities to their field. Newey's curiosity in racing cars deepened when he was trying to understand "why people in other areas [e.g., architecture, aircraft design] do what they do and then see what you can reapply in your field."[18]

Unlearn the Habits That You Created, and Move Forward

We need to condition ourselves to this constant state of curiosity with a willingness to unlearn, Michael Jager told me. "You have to be willing to say, 'You know what, everybody loved those graphics and that thing last year, but we've got to kill that. We have to kill what we know worked and move forward.' And I always would reference the Clash. You look at every single album that the Clash or the Beatles did. What those guys were doing was learning and moving. Learning and moving."[19]

Don't Settle

Continue to investigate different ways to approach your field. Your drive for curiosity should lead you to much experimentation. Create the time to hone that skill set. Remember that finding your style, voice, signature, or authorship too early may be a pitfall. You'll want to experiment with different product concepts, different routes to your destination, different writing styles, different material, and so forth. Settling on an approach too early will deprive you of exciting new possibilities that you couldn't have even imagined at first.

Remain an Enfant Terrible

As we grow older and accumulate more knowledge, we tend to acquire more emotional grounding and become better at assessing the mood of the listener, but we also tend not to push when we feel that doing so is getting us nowhere. Revive your enfant terrible. Ask questions, challenge everything, and don't feel trapped by conventions, regardless of the audience. I have a friend who is completely mad about cycling and asks endless questions to improve his performance: What kind of diet is appropriate, or even how to cut his hair for aerodynamics. Sometimes his questions alienate others, who think this is all a bit too much, but little does he care. When he explains his passion and drive for success, he typically wins them back.

Revamp the Team

Every time you add more people to your team and enhance your capabilities, you become stronger and better able to tackle new frontiers and solve new mysteries, Sekiyama told me. "We've continually been growing ever since we first started the project, and every time we have some small success, and every time we add more people to our team, every time we grow in terms of capabilities, there just becomes more and more things that we become able to tackle."[20] If you are going in a new direction in your field, you need different people. Say you've been making sports clothing all your life and now you want to delve deeper into smart clothing— wearables that track your steps or monitor your body temperature. You will most likely need to add a software developer to your team to go further with your idea.

Path B: Exit the Current Field, and Branch Out to a New One

Rob Nail was born in a small agricultural town outside Sacramento, California. His mother nurtured his curiosity from an early age. She would take Rob and his siblings to the library and encourage them to choose any books they wanted. "We did this every weekend," he said, "and we could bring as many books home as we could carry. That was the rule. There was a weight condition on that. So if you wanted one big art book, that's all you got if that's all you could manage."[21] This habit helped open the world to Nail as he explored many topics through those library books. "Because I had to sit with that same book for a whole week, I flipped through the whole thing. It wasn't like reading the summary paragraph that you get in a tweet or whatever you get today on the internet." Instead of focusing on pulling one thread, Nail would end up with multiple threads, each with its own story and potential. "The more your experiences take you into the depths of some topics, the broader the universe unfolds for you."

Nail graduated from a high school in Sacramento, and only three in his class went on to college.[22] He was accepted at the University of California, Davis, where he studied engineering.

There he met his best friend, JoeBen Bevirt. They shared a common interest: flying cars. "We had both heard about this gentleman named Paul Moller, who was at UC Davis," Nail said. "He had an honorary aeronautical PhD, building a flying car. We ended up interning at his little thing, and it was like a playground where we could just explore and look for new things. So, I found another universe where I could dig into and play."[23] Nail continued to work at Moller International after graduation while Bevirt went to graduate school at Stanford University. In one of his visits to Stanford, Nail became curious about what his friend and others were working on. "It opened up this other world that I had not realized existed as well, which is Palo Alto, California, this Silicon Valley thing, which is a whole other universe entirely." Convinced by Bevirt, Nail applied to graduate school and was accepted.

Graduate school opened up another intriguing universe for Nail. It was in the late 1990s, when the dot-com boom was exploding in Silicon Valley. "The internet thing made no sense to me at all," Nail remembered. "I just figured I would build robots and focus on that side of technology. I was also moonlighting with my friend JoeBen, who was working at a pharmaceutical company at the time, helping researchers improve their process. That was fun, helping these scientists who were doing cool stuff."

Nail and Bevirt realized that there was enormous potential for what they were doing. They managed to spin out into starting Velocity11, a life-science robotics company, in 1999. They went from bootstrapping to growing their venture and selling it to Agilent Technologies, where Nail stayed for a couple of years.

After satisfying this interest, Nail went looking for his next big thing. He felt that he had exhausted this domain and became curious about growing start-ups. He grew intrigued by angel investing, which presented him with another steep learning curve. During that time, Nail says he would swing between uncertainty and enthusiasm. "That's when I met the engineer, doctor, and entrepreneur, Peter Diamandis," Nail recalled. "He and Ray Kurzweil, the American inventor and futurist, had just started Singularity University, which offers executive educational programs, business incubation, and innovation consultancy. I attended its first executive program. I walked in thinking I was an expert in robotics and biotech. In that week, I was learning about things happening in robotics and biotech I didn't realize were happening. That was exciting."[24] Nail became interested in how breakthroughs happening in the parallel spaces of neuroscience and nanotech were overlapping in the robotics business that he had built. It represented a thrilling new horizon for him.

Nail was so taken by Singularity University that after more than a decade in the robotics industry, he was excited to continue to explore new strides in this domain. He invested time and money in the field and created several ideas for the university founders to pursue. Diamandis and Kurzweil were impressed. "It was very exciting," Nail said. "I had started by helping out and advising but ended up taking over about a year later to run and then to become the CEO of Singularity University."[25] Nail had found his new purpose.

Like Nail, we have to understand that at some point in our lives, we will turn our curiosity in a different direction. Instead of being a passenger in the vehicle of change, we will jump into the driver's seat to be creative and branch out into new domains. One day, we may stop being interested in unearthing treasures in the same field. Once we achieve what we had set out to do and reach the summit, our level of curiosity about the field might diminish. The good news is that there will always be another chapter. If we have reached the peak in this area, now is the time to stop and move on to other things.

So, how can we set ourselves up for a new curiosity journey in a new field? How do we make the transition from one area to a new one? Because people are living longer, acquiring new knowledge and skills, and retiring later, it seems likely that we will have two, three, or even more careers over our working lives. Yet switching fields may feel daunting. Here are some strategies to get it right.

Kill What You Know

Serial entrepreneur Roberta Lucca, who has moved into different domains, referred to David Bowie as her role model. "Bowie was not afraid of being original, killing the characters that he built successfully and starting again, because he thought there was something new to bring to the world," Lucca said.[26] "He said, 'I'm going to kill Ziggy Stardust to start something new and I'm fine with that. I'm going to move on, and hopefully that will encourage more people to do the same thing in their own lives.'"

Create the Space for New Inspiration to Enter Your Life

Go down different rabbit holes that you daydream about. Now is not the time to overthink. Just go with your curiosity, and evaluate where you are along the way. Video game developer, artist, and professor Auriea Harvey, whom we met earlier in the book, explained, "I would just lose myself in the thoughts about what we could develop next."[27] It doesn't matter how outlandish or unrealistic it seems—in fact, the more far-out the better. Loosen your grip on what's possible, and don't confine your ideas. Now is the time to let ideas flow.

Find Your New Purpose

Going down different rabbit holes is about finding a new sense of purpose, becoming the owner of something new. Fall in love with your next idea as soon as you have reached your last goal. Start dreaming of new endeavors without skimping on current resources and attention for your current project. Don't lose sight of where you go. Jess Butcher, a London-based technology entrepreneur, angel investor, and nonexecutive director for start-ups, has a demonstrable track record of building successful businesses from scratch over the last fifteen years. She noted that what she wants to do now is very different from the tech start-ups she founded and the investments she made in the past. She aspires to start a movement that focuses on mental health issues. "It is about developing a genuinely useful tool for anyone in the world that is motivating them," she explained.[28]

Carve Time to Acquire Information and Resources in the New Domain

Tencia Lee, the aforementioned hedge fund trader who came up with an algorithm to diagnose heart disease from MRI images, explained how excited she had been to learn about machine learning after being in finance for six years: "I thought, 'I don't want to stay in this area. I don't think there's much here for me that will be very interesting anymore.' Otherwise, it would have been hard to put forward the level of concentrated effort that it took to learn all this. But at the same time, as soon as I started doing it, I thought I was very glad to be doing it and that I wanted to know more."[29]

Be Kind to Yourself, and Leap

Repeat after me: "My plan so far worked nicely, but I have exhausted my curiosity and now I'm going to explore another shiny object in a new field, start from scratch, and if it goes down a road I never anticipated, that's fine." Switching into a different field, getting curious about other things, is OK. Something that we were curious about five years ago may seem kind of boring to us now. So, it is absolutely normal to grow curious about a new field.

> *Instead of being a passenger in the vehicle of change, we will jump in the driver's seat to be creative and branch out into new domains.*

EVERYTHING IN MODERATION

Whatever path you decide to take (as with everything else in life), it may be wise to engage with curiosity in moderation—neither too little nor too much. Some of the people I interviewed for this book often warned of dangerous extremes and how taking their purposeful curiosity too far proved counterproductive or had otherwise negative implications for their personal lives. They talked about paying a high personal price to pursue their curiosity journeys. Many have deferred taking holidays or were unable to always be there for their families or other loved ones, missing important events, losing sleep, having their partners or family members complain about the time they spent on their curiosity journeys.

Ancient Greeks believed that one should live one's life by choosing the middle ground and should avoid extremes as much as possible. The maxim pan metron ariston (παν μέτρον άριστον)—"everything in moderation"—coined by Greek poet Cleobulus of Lindos in the sixth century BC, is essential to our purposefully curious journeys. There is a way to achieve great things and satisfy your curiosity while also finding balance, enjoying life, and taking care of yourself.

First, remind yourself about your *long-term purpose*, what drives you. You need to ask yourself endlessly, "What is my aim? What am I working for?" Beware of going down a rabbit hole mindlessly; you need to consider your long-term purpose, the broader picture. Go down the rabbit hole because of your purpose, your broader road map, said H. William "Bill" Harlan, the founder and owner of Napa Valley's iconic Harlan Estate.[30] A short-term focus discourages moderation. Our ability to adapt and focus our curiosity doesn't improve when we spend more time scrolling greedily through website after website. Doing so may make us feel good in the short run. Yet, uncontrolled, this habit can scale up to an unhealthy level and prevent us from making substantive, measurable progress. Without realizing it, we may discount our long-term interest. I am not anti-tech at all. Cutting out technology from our lives is also problematic. But to push beyond what is known, we have to remember that we must also be producers, not only consumers. By adopting a long-term-purpose mindset, we are forced to better allocate our attention, time, and resources.

Second, become *mindful* about when enough is enough, and put on the brakes before the indulgence quickly spirals into dangerous and unsatisfying territory. Staying there longer may make it harder to come back. In other words, pay attention while you are going all in. What triggers this constant craving for new surprises or challenging tasks? Is it boredom or the fear of stillness, for example, that causes these habits? Reflecting on these questions will give you something valuable. We need to become more mindful to understand why we do what we do and what course of action is needed to keep perspective. By being more aware of what is driving us, we can more easily return to the desired middle ground. If you are neglecting family and friends, for example, can you readjust your schedule to accommodate time for them? Can you replace screen time while walking to work with looking at buildings or observing what people do, read, or wear instead?

Third, *pick a partner in crime*, and listen to them when possible. A partner (a family member, a friend, or a trusted colleague from work) can make you accountable and keep you in check. They can call you out to bring you back to the present moment. The role of an accountability partner is critical, Olympic medalist Nicole Cooke told me. "Many times, the coach was absolutely right—I did need to ease off, but sometimes I had to learn by bad experiences."[31] Being on your own can often lead to careless overdoing, so listen to other people's perspectives.

While a student at the University of California, Berkeley, Harlan fell in love with Napa Valley, the renowned winery region about fifty miles north of San Francisco.[32] He started dreaming of owning a vineyard. Harlan continued visiting the region, tasting wine, delving deeper into winemaking, and keeping ahead of developments in the area. In 1975, he cofounded Pacific Union Company, a real estate development firm that converted apartments to condominiums.[33] Harlan and his cofounder, Peter Stocker, built the firm into one of the largest commercial and residential property developers in the United States. His success enabled him to buy Meadowood, a run-down country club in St. Helena, Napa County, which he transformed into an iconic retreat.[34] In 1980, Robert Mondavi, the renowned Californian vintner who put Napa Valley on the world map, became interested in establishing the Auction Napa Valley, a charity auction that distributes proceeds to local nonprofits and strategic initiatives and is modeled after the Hospices de Beaune.[35] The event would take place at Harlan's Meadowood resort.

Mondavi asked Harlan to join him on a trip to France.[36] They visited all the great châteaus at Bordeaux and the grands crus at Burgundy.[37] In his book, *Observations from the Hillside*, Harlan explains about how seeing these estates and meeting the families that sustained their own legacies throughout time converted his interest into a new curiosity project with a purpose.[38] His ambition became to create a Napa first growth, which would mean producing one of the finest Bordeaux-style reds on the planet, along the lines of Mouton Rothschild and Latour.[39] This goal also changed his perspective about time: from the short-term focus of a real estate developer who jumped from one project to the next to that of a person building something that would last for many generations.[40]

Harlan started learning about winemaking, tapping into the wisdom of established winemaking families and examining how he could break away from what had already been done in Napa Valley.[41] He wrote detailed notes and painstakingly dissected the secrets of dynastic longevity.[42] Inspired by what he saw in Europe, Harlan developed a two-hundred-year plan and dipped his toes into this new field by starting a small winery, building an outstanding team of experts, and releasing its first vintage in 1983.[43] He founded Harlan Estate in 1984 by acquiring the first forty acres of uncultivated land in the hills above Oakville, Napa County.[44] Harlan spent four decades building Harlan Estate into a brand that effortlessly sells at double the price of a Bordeaux first growth and launching other successful labels like the Bond and Promontory wineries, along with the famed Meadowood Resort and the Napa Valley Reserve. "We won't ever be done," Harlan told a reporter.[45]

Purposeful curiosity is a love affair, not a one-night stand. It's a big world, and there are many places where no one has been; there are still many discoveries to be made in every area of study. You could live until you are one hundred, and you'd still just be finding your way around. Being purposefully curious is about being constantly inquisitive, acquiring new knowledge and experiences, and questioning what you've done before. Your curiosity can make a positive difference, and it is pleasurable to be in a constant state of motion.

Channeling our curiosity to push boundaries is the essence of life. Whether that love affair is about discovering new places worth exploring or even new planets to visit is up to you. When we feel that we have satisfied our curiosity or that future projects will no longer bring us closer to our initial goals, it may be time to reevaluate what we are doing. It may be time to get excited about new fields.

I am confident that we will never run out of new things to explore. But at the same time, we must be creative, willing to learn, and open to branching out into different areas. Be mindful, stay passionate, and, above all, remain curious.

– THE TAKEAWAYS –

- Reaching the summit of your curiosity journey is a big deal. Take time to be grateful for everything that you have accomplished before moving on to explore the next horizon. Turn the ending of one curiosity project into the beginning of a new one.
- Three common challenges may impede your pioneering spirit once your curiosity is satisfied:
  - » The anticlimax that follows the high of satisfying your curiosity
  - » The struggle to find a bigger challenge to conquer, or becoming overwhelmed by the endless possibilities
  - » Reaching the destination may turn off your curiosity

- Reflecting on your completed curiosity project or projects, you have to ask yourself one crucial question: "Am I still curious about exploring this field?" Depending on your answer, there are two directions that you can take:
  - » Path A: You are still excited about your chosen field. Stay the course, and continue stretching the boundaries of your chosen field.

> » Path B: You feel that you have exhausted this field, and you are keen to find a new one to explore. Exit the current area, and branch out to a curiosity journey in a new area.

- Whatever path you decide to take (as with everything else in life), curiosity may be best when experienced in moderation. Beware of the dangers of excess!

Afterword

> *Therein lies the true source of curiosity and*
> *wonder: the not knowing—coupled with its*
> *only antidote, the need to know.*
>
> —NEIL DEGRASSE TYSON, COSMIC QUERIES

AS I EMERGED FROM THIS LENGTHY YET REWARDING JOURNEY RESEARCH-
ing and writing about purposeful curiosity, my life had changed in
fundamental ways. Having a purpose that I was passionate about
has made it easier to spend more time working on the book. I realized that when I am deeply engaged in work, my energy increases.
I also realized that I had to act on my passion rather than perpetually daydream about it. My relationship with technology has
improved. To satisfy my own curiosity and push beyond what I
know, I have started paying attention to the things that matter to
my work. The pendulum has swung back from mindlessly scrolling
the internet in my downtime to finding something interesting to
focus on and embracing the road less traveled. My own experience

makes it very clear: now is the time to rekindle and protect the practice of purposeful curiosity, because time is finite.

As I walked the streets of London playing with different ideas on how to finish this book, I kept thinking that I was almost done. I shared everything I knew with you. Then it hit me. I still have a lot of work to do. All of us still have a lot of work to do. Let me close with some thoughts and suggestions on how we can successfully unlock purposeful curiosity in our parenting, education, and society.

> *Our journeys can have a great impact on society and make our world a safer, healthier, happier, more ingenious, and empathetic place.*

PARENTING

As a child, my daughter, Lydia, was insatiably curious about her surroundings, constantly investigating, experimenting, and observing. We were living in a small, cozy apartment in central London at that time, and she was always so enthusiastic about our pots and pans and constantly asking numerous *why* questions. Being curious myself, I never found her questions annoying or exhausting, even when she reached a point in her development where the word *why* was her response to just about everything my wife or I didn't know the answer to. I thought that this thirst for answers was natural. She wanted to understand the world around her. When we took her to nearby gardens and parks, she picked flowers, turned rocks over, and conducted nonstop mini-experiments. From early on, I realized that kids are born scientists and that everything they do is about exploring and testing.

Lydia reminded me of myself when I was a child. Like Lydia, I had this incredible curiosity, but I also had a terrible habit (terrible, as far as my parents were concerned) of taking things apart. There was never a toy I would not unscrew. Nor were appliances and computers safe from my inquisitive hands, for that matter. I had one goal in mind: to reveal their inner workings. I was the ultimate deconstructor. Imagine the shock of my parents when they realized that many of the things that they had bought me were no longer working. Reflecting on my childhood years, I am so grateful to my parents, who never had a serious conversation with me about this habit of mine but who, on the contrary, casually and subtly became my loyal patrons, supporting as much as they could my next deconstruction experiments. It was beautiful growing up in a family where I was encouraged to open things, understand how they worked, and try to improve them or combine them with other things.

My curiosity kingdom was toys, tools, and, yes, a lot of junk. I was reluctant to part with my collections of bits and pieces, since I always believed that one of them could prove valuable for my next experiment. I was drawn to infinite possibilities and mysteries, problems and puzzles, catalysts for imagination. As a child, I also had numerous interests—technology, art, design, architecture, music, and business—and always found exploratory questions about the future very appealing (e.g., "What comes next?"). As I got a little older, my diverse interests, along with my inclination toward the unknown, made me an avid reader. I spent most of my pocket money on magazines and newspapers. My local newsstand and my school's library were my version of the internet. I was always converting my interests into projects to investigate further. My parents encouraged my curiosity instead of finding it annoying and frustrating.

So how can we nurture our children's purposeful curiosity?

Help Children Develop a Curious Attitude

We must inspire children to ask hard questions rather than stamping on them. Hazel Forsyth, the senior curator at the Museum of London, recalled, "I remember having an encyclopedia that my mum gave me. And in the front, there was a drawing, and I think it's a verse by Kipling, and it says, 'I keep six honest serving-men (they taught me all I knew); their names are What and Why and When and How and Where and Who.'"[1] Award-winning crime fiction author Michael Robotham highlighted the superpower of "What if you were . . . ?" questions: "Again, this is the ultimate act of empathy, anyway, to put yourself in someone else's shoes, you know. And people should do it more often. What if you were a refugee? Let's explore that because what do you think would happen if . . . ?"[2]

Throwing those sorts of questions at children and getting them to think about their answers inspires curiosity. When they ask you about the way their toys work, about electricity, or about how the vacuum cleaner works, you need to take their questions seriously. Leda Braga, the hedge fund manager and CEO of Systematica Investments, offered great advice: "I always tried to give the most complete answer possible. If you don't know, then you may say, 'You ought to go and read about this, because this is the limit of what I know. I don't know any more.'"[3]

Encourage Children to Launch Their Own Purposeful Curiosity Projects

Ask kids to be curious about topics that they feel passionate about. Anything goes: They might conceive of new worlds, learn more about what their parents do for a living, or imagine how their projects can have a positive impact on the world. The beauty is that their motivation will help them understand unknown phenomena and help them become competent learners.

Set a Good Example

There's nothing more frustrating than a distracted parent scrolling through a smartphone. "Be curious about your children, their views," said Zar Amrolia of XTX Markets.[4] Children have invaluable information on the latest trends. Listen and be prepared to be wowed by everything that you will learn from them. Talk to your children about your own curiosity projects. Show them part of your research, some preliminary findings, prototypes—whatever you have. Capture their interest visually and tactilely. Sharing good curiosity habits with your children goes a long way in establishing lifelong curiosity.

Get Curious Together

Find a mystery that you and your child want to solve together. For example, race car engineer Adrian Newey explained to me how helping his father, a veterinary surgeon who was also a great amateur engineer and car enthusiast, build a car from a kit got him interested in cars and car design.[5] Teach your child how to build something, how not to expect everything to be given to them in life, and how to pick up the toolbox and try to make it themselves before they ask someone else to do it for them. Involving the child and then occasionally leaving them alone gives them time to seek information, experiment, and learn and, perhaps more importantly, nurtures their self-sufficiency, that useful characteristic that the ancient Greeks called *autarkia*. It is about giving kids the space to be on their own so that they can discover what they need, take care of themselves, and avoid self-pity.

EDUCATION

My job as an educator is to make my topics inspiring and interesting, to actively protect the spirit of inquiry, and to give my students fascinating mysteries to examine. Academics are paid to be purposefully curious. We conduct research on, and teach in, areas that spark our interest, and we often spend long periods exploring different research questions. Being allowed to work on different puzzles as an adult is a remarkable privilege. We should celebrate lifelong learning. Understanding the context and always being up-to-date with the latest knowledge prepares us to face any new challenge that comes our way.

What can we do to educate a new generation of students so that they maintain a state of healthy doubt, actively and purposefully explore, do their own research, and welcome the unknown? The people I interviewed offered intriguing advice.

Turn students from passive recipients of information to curious owners of their learning journey, advised John Underkoffler, the previously mentioned cofounder of Oblong Industries.[6] We must encourage students to delve deeper into topics that spark their curiosity. Curating relevant information will enhance their confidence and incite curiosity in others when they share their newly discovered insights with the rest of the class.

Create a safe atmosphere where students can "put their hands up and ask questions," said investor Edward Bonham Carter.[7] I was fortunate because the school that I attended as a student encouraged a Socratic approach to learning. The method involved meaningful conversations with our teachers, who navigated the subjects by answering many questions. Nothing was out-of-bounds—there were no stupid questions. Education should invite students to question authority and not to unquestioningly accept ideas fed to us by the media, government, or big business. Serial entrepreneur

Jess Butcher recommended inviting students to debate and open a dialogue about their findings.[8] This approach can create entirely new insights.

Encourage students to work on projects that align with their interests and give them time, said Brightworks founder Gever Tulley.[9] Empowered students working on their own or in teams feel entirely and unapologetically themselves. When given time and space, students push boundaries they didn't know existed and are inspired to search for answers. Fostering a systematic and protracted approach ensures that they will dissect the latest studies, frameworks, tools, videos, and images.

Polar explorer Ben Saunders noted that students and other people learn by experiencing things.[10] Education must create opportunities where students directly experience their surroundings, embrace uncertainty, and welcome the unknown. Hands-on experiments, inspiration-gathering trips, and other adventures all fuel creativity; they lead to exciting discoveries and mobilize meaningful connections. If they must work as a team, students can learn to help each other so that they can achieve a common goal.

SOCIETY

We should endorse the successful unlocking of purposeful curiosity in our society at large. The mark of a civilized society is the way it treats curious people. A barbaric society punishes them; a civilized society embraces and appreciates them. Change holds seeds for good. Every time life throws challenges at us, we should perceive them as opportunities for growth. We must become more curious, get to know ourselves better, ask new questions and seek answers, reach out to new like-minded people, daydream freely, pursue new ideas, and aim for a positive impact on others. Where there is a purposeful curiosity project, there is hope. Progress has always depended on curiosity. Curiosity helps us work toward improving what we already do, set higher standards, and achieve more-challenging goals. CEO Don Wilson says that to evolve in everything we do, we must keep pace with change and avoid standing still.[11] Encouraging and maintaining our curiosity as a society is the only way to continue looking ahead. To make a difference, curiosity journeys need to not only be successful but also have purpose.

It would be ironic if we failed to nourish and protect this superpower just when we increasingly recognize its value. As a society, we must do our best to hold on to our curiosity as we get older. We must resist the urge to become fixed in our ways as we grow older. There is no reason to become boring and respectable and to blend into the background just because doing so seems more appropriate at a certain age. We have to remain interested in everything and everyone.

Society should echo Nietzsche's thesis that a fulfilling life requires embracing rather than running from difficulty. As a society, we must nurture purposeful curiosity, using any means we can.

First, we must bring back the spirit of exploration, says eco-explorer Raphaël Domjan. Also important is the essence of surprise, added Georgianna Hiliadaki, the chef and cofounder of a two-Michelin-star restaurant.[12] Like Jacques Cousteau, the great explorer who traveled the world with his research vessel *Calypso* exploring ocean life in original and inspiring ways, we must be motivated by mysteries that pique our interest.

Things that make us uncomfortable help us grow. Caleb Kramer, a Los Angeles–based strategy director, shared this advice: If we want to have long-lasting, fulfilling lives, we should open our minds by focusing our curiosity on things that capture our attention.[13] Our relentless curiosity should drive us "to question everything we see, asking why something has happened, or not to take things too much for granted," said Max Mersch, a venture capitalist in decentralized networks.[14] We must get inspired by other fields and participate in interdisciplinary discussions and forums. Or we can simply go outside and stop living vicariously through other people. Hiliadaki said that purposeful curiosity is also about incorporating everything that we learn to create a surprise. "In the restaurant," she explained, "some customers eat their dishes first, and then we reveal what they have eaten. This is the essence of surprise. We create a mystery. Even from the title of the dish, you do not understand what it is. In the social media, we upload a photo without describing the ingredients, so that the customers [must] have the curiosity to try it."[15]

The message is clear. We have to target our curiosity while embracing our inner four-year-old. That is, we need curiosity in abundance—the ability to stay interested in a topic for as long as it can yield new qualities and inspiration.

A final important step we must take is to move from *I* to *we*. By perpetually stretching the boundaries of knowledge, we leave positive impacts in our world. A change-the-world idealism can be received with skepticism, though. Curiosity hasn't always been highly prized. After all, curiosity was what kicked Adam and Eve out of the Garden of Eden. In the 1600s, Blaise Pascal, the famous French mathematician and philosopher, described curiosity as "only vanity. We usually only want to know something so that we can talk about it."[16] One may argue that purposeful curiosity journeys resemble elaborate self-indulgent vanity projects. At some level, they may be. But every time we pull them off, we create a legacy. Success is always an important motivator. But it is not what drives these projects. Our journeys can greatly benefit society, making our world a safer, healthier, happier, more ingenious, and empathetic place.

For Ma Yansong, the award-winning architect and founder of Beijing-based MAD Architects, whose designs blend into nature, his work makes the world a better place. "I think what is more difficult is to create something meaningful for the future or more positive," he said. "When I watch science fiction movies, I really don't like very dark and high-density urban scenes. Future solutions should solve the problems that we are facing now. If we have some problems, we don't want them to continue into the future. So, future solutions should solve issues. Then, when we create something for the future, it's full of love. We are hoping the future is very caring for the people."[17]

There is nothing more inspiring than seeing people, teams, and organizations pushing to do things that have never been done before and maximizing their contribution back to society. We are inspired when people do high-quality work for the betterment of society and not just for the benefit of a small segment of people. Polar expeditions, for instance, combine science and adventure. They serve as a laboratory for testing human dynamics, and scientists have used Antarctic explorations to test space suits for use on Mars. Curiosity journeys promote progress. They allow us to be better than we imagine we can be. We must also share with others the knowledge we gain from our journeys. We must mentor others, support their curiosity journeys, and share our knowledge with our team members. Pause and think, "What is the bigger picture? What is the relevance of my curiosity project? How can my curiosity journey help other people face their challenges or achieve their aspirations? How can I have a positive impact on other people?" This won't be a sprint. It will be a marathon.

WHAT ARE YOU WAITING FOR?

We glamorize people who push boundaries. We often also assume that their efforts are beyond comprehension by us mere mortals. I hope that by taking you behind the scenes on a tour of the so-called Curiosity Galápagos—home to individuals who engage in a directed form of exploration, stretch the boundaries of their fields, reach their goals, and start over again—you have learned ways to focus and exercise your curiosity. Purposeful curiosity can help us harness the power to supercharge learning, break bad habits, and live happier, more engaged lives.

When you put down this book, I hope that the lessons, insights, tips, and stories I've shared leave you with an urge to be purposefully curious. Some of the stories I've shared resemble the American dream or a Hollywood blockbuster. But they are not just meant to entertain us; they are meant to rally us. On the one hand, the protagonists of amazing curiosity journeys are full of hope to push beyond what is known and discover new territory. On the other hand, they also face challenges that they must overcome. They experience setbacks and often end up broken. Yet, remarkably, they recover and carry on until they reach their destination. Curiosity journeys are about willpower, success, and a belief in happy endings.

Purposeful curiosity is significant for humanity. It has always been, and it's even more so today. To protect people, protect life on this planet, and benefit society in the short and long term, we can embrace curiosity to make a big difference. We shouldn't feel beholden to our pasts. We evolve, and our journeys do, too.

By being more purposefully curious about our ever-changing planet, we can rewrite and update its manual with every discovery. Don't wait for permission. Ask more from your life (we, allegedly, only get one). Pay attention to your itch, and go for it now! Together, we will encounter no limit to what we can achieve.

Appendices
and Resources

Appendix of Interviews

Louis Alderson-Bythell   Director, Lvboratory
Lecturer in Bio-Design, Royal College of Art

Dr. Zar Amrolia, PhD   Co-CEO, XTX Markets

Dr. Anand Anandkumar,   Cofounder and CEO, Bugworks
PhD

Felicity Aston   Polar Explorer, Royal Geographical Society
Fellow, The Explorers Club

Lionel Barber   Journalist and Former Editor, *Financial Times*

Peter Beck   Founder and CEO, Rocket Lab

Sam Bompas   Cofounder and Director, Bompas & Parr Studio

Edward Bonham Carter   Director of Stewardship and Corporate Responsibility,
Jupiter Asset Management

Pete Bottomley   Cofounder and Studio Head, White Paper Games

Leda Braga   CEO, Systematica Investments

Zowie Broach   Head of Fashion, Royal College of Art
Cofounder, Boudicca

Vern Brownell   Technology and Business Consultant, Next Step
Technology Consulting
Former CEO, D-Wave Systems

Maximilian Büsser	Owner and Creative Director, MB&F
Jess Butcher, MBE	Entrepreneur, Angel Invester Adviser, Equality and Human Rights Non-Executive Commissioner
Nicole Cooke, MBE	Olympic Champion Strategy Manager, Swiss Re
Marshall Culpepper	Director of Off-world Applications, Filecoin Foundation Cofounder and Former CEO, KubOS
Giampaolo Dallara	Founder and President, Dallara Group
Raphaël Domjan	Eco-adventurer and Speaker (www.raphaeldomjan.com)
Raviv Drucker	Journalist, Political Commentator, and Investigative Journalist
John Fawcett	Director of Product Management, Robinhood
Hazel Forsyth	Senior Curator (Post-Medieval), Museum of London
Lord Norman Foster	Founder and Executive Chairman, Foster + Partners President, Norman Foster Foundation
Martin Frost, CBE	Chair and Cofounder, Monumo Chair, Peek Vision and Sorex Sensors Former CEO, CMR Surgical
Charles Gordon-Lennox	11th Duke of Richmond, Goodwood Estate
Raia Hadsell	Senior Research Scientist, Google DeepMind
H. William Harlan	Founder, Harlan Estate
Auriea Harvey	Professor of Games, Kunsthochschule Kassel (Kassel University, School of Fine Arts, Germany) Artist-Sculptor, Auriea Harvey Studio
Thieme Hennis	Researcher, AstroPlant Entrepreneur, And the People
Georgianna Hiliadaki	Chef and Cofounder, Funky Gourmet, Opso, Ino, Pittabun
Håkon Høydal	Journalist, *Verdens Gang*
Dr. Roger Ibbotson, PhD	Chairman and CIO, Zebra Capital Management Professor, Yale School of Management
Daisy Jacobs	Animator, Writer, Director (www.thebiggerpicturefilm.com)

Michael Jager	Chief Creative Officer, Solidarity of Unbridled Labour
Mary Katrantzou	Fashion Designer (www.marykatrantzou.com)
George Kourounis	Adventurer, Storm Chaser, TV Presenter (www .stormchaser.ca/)
Caleb Kramer	Strategy Director, AKQA
Tencia Lee	Staff Machine Learning Engineer, Cruise Automation
Brett Lovelady	Founder and Partner, Astro Studios (PA Consulting)
Roberta Lucca	Cofounder, Bossa Studios
	Founder, Creative Director and Host, Hyper Curious Podcast
	YouTube Channel Creator and Host, Betta Lucca
Max Mersch	Cofounder and Partner, Fabric Ventures
Rob Nail	Associate Founder, Faculty Member, and Former CEO, Singularity University
Sean Ness	Business Development Director, Institute for the Future
Adrian Newey	Chief Technical Officer, Red Bull Racing
Olly Olsen	Cofounder and Co-CEO, The Office Group
Dr. Claudia Pasquero, PhD	Cofounder and Director, ecoLogicStudio
	Associate Professor and Director of the Urban Morphogenesis Lab, The Bartlett, University College London
	Landscape Architecture Professor, Head of IOUD (Institute of Urban Design), and Director of the Synthetic Landscape Lab, Innsbruck University
Yonatan Raz-Fridman	Founder and CEO, Supersocial
	Cofounder and Former CEO, Kano Computing
Chen Reiss	Soprano (www.chenreiss.com)
Michael Robotham	Author (www.michaelrobotham.com)
Ben Saunders	Polar Explorer, Endurance Athlete, Keynote Speaker, Climate Tech Investor (www.bensaunders.com)
Dr. Jacques Schuhmacher, PhD	Rosalinde and Arthur Gilbert Provenance Curator, Victoria & Albert Museum
Kazuhide Sekiyama	Director and Representative Executive Officer, Spiber

Ceylan Shevket	Head of Creatures/Creature Supervisor, One of Us VFX
Gershon Tenenbaum	Professor, Florida State University
Nigel Toon	Cofounder and CEO, Graphcore
Gever Tulley	Founder and Codirector, Brightworks School Founder, Tinkering School
Gavin Turk	Artist (www.gavinturk.com)
John Underkoffler	Principal, Treadle & Loam, Provisioners Former CEO, Oblong Industries
Jólan van der Wiel	Designer (jolanvanderwiel.com)
Dr. Angelo Vermeulen, Ph.D.	Researcher, Delft University of Technology
Jon Wiley	On Sabbatical, Former Senior Director, Google
Don Wilson	Founder and CEO, DRW
Ma Yansong	Founder and Principal Partner, MAD Architects

Acknowledgments

I OWE DEEP THANKS TO MANY PEOPLE, WITHOUT WHOM *PURPOSEFUL Curiosity* wouldn't have been possible. First and most obviously, I would like to start by thanking all the curious people featured in this book for sharing their wisdom so that we can learn from their experiences. I truly appreciate your help. You are all an inspiration.

Publishing this book has been a real joy. I would like to thank my editors, Lauren Marino (Hachette) and Liz Gough (Yellow Kite Books), for their support and enthusiasm throughout this project. I feel a strong sense of gratitude to them for believing in the power of purposeful curiosity. They have been instrumental in shepherding this book through the development process and ensuring it's the very best it can be. Thanks also to the rest of the teams at Hachette and Yellow Kite Books, in production, marketing, publicity, sales, and rights, among others, as well as to Jack Ramm for his early editorial work and Karen Kelly for her invaluable and intelligent editing of the book. Karen's huge help made the book stronger than it would have been without her considerable expertise and skill. It has been a privilege to work with you, Karen.

Throughout the process of researching and writing this book, many friends generously shared their precious time and helped with ideas, read-throughs, points of contact. I would like to thank Iraklis Zisimopoulos, Sophia Papastathi, Valia Anyfioti, David Roche, Lito Pitiris, Philippos Kassimatis, Dimitris Papageorgiou, Marianne Lewis, Andre Spicer, Caroline Wiertz, Ruben van Werven, Ella Miron-Spektor, Spencer Harrison, George Athanasopoulos, Alexander Macridis, and Virna Kallia. I am also grateful to Chrysa Gotsi, Chrysanthi Bimpiri, and Eleni Karaiskou for all their research assistance with this book. I am very sorry if I forgot anybody.

Over the past eight years, I've had the great pleasure of being a member of Bayes Business School at City, University of London. Bayes really promotes intellectual curiosity. I would like to thank all my colleagues and students at Bayes for being so supportive, and for providing such an intellectually stimulating place to work. Without your support I could not have researched and written this book.

A big thank-you to my agent, Ben Clark at the Soho Agency. He has been a great friend and indispensable in helping to develop the idea for this book, capably helping me to navigate the world of publishing, reading my work, and talking through my ideas. I can't imagine a better agent.

Most of all, I am grateful to my mother and father, Mary and Apostolos, who have been tirelessly supportive of my curious pursuits. Thank you for teaching me by example to work hard, have a ton of questions, and be original. It is thanks to you that I have an unbridled sense of exploration. It is your kindness and care that helped shape me into the person I am today. I miss you both.

Last but certainly not least, my greatest thanks to my beloved wife, Manto, and my daughter, Lydia, for their endless understanding, patience, and love. Writing this book was especially challenging, and without their support, I simply could not have done it. Thank you, Manto, for all your help with reading various versions of the book. Every time we are together, I feel energized. Lydia, thank you for being so curious. I owe all the good things in my life to both of you. To our next explorations!

Notes

PREFACE

1. T. B. Kashdan and P. J. Silvia, "Curiosity and Interest: The Benefits of Thriving on Novelty and Challenge," in *The Oxford Handbook of Positive Psychology*, 2nd ed., ed. S. J. Lopez, and C. R. Snyder (Oxford, UK: Oxford University Press, 2009), 367–374; J. A. Litman, T. L. Hutchins, and R. K. Russon, "Epistemic Curiosity, Feeling-of-Knowing, and Exploratory Behaviour," *Cognition & Emotion* 19, no. 4 (2005): 559–582.

2. Jacquelyn Bulao, "How Much Data Is Created Every Day in 2021?," *Techjury*, January 4, 2022, https://techjury.net/blog/how-much-data-is-created-every-day/#gref.

3. Maryam Mohsin, "10 Google Search Statistics You Need to Know in 2021," *Oberlo*, April 2, 2020, www.oberlo.com/blog/google-search-statistics.

4. Barry Schwartz, "Google Reaffirms 15% of Searches Are New, Never Been Searched Before," *Search Engine Land*, April 25, 2017, https://search engineland.com/google-reaffirms-15-searches-new-never-searched-273786.

5. Georgiev Deyan, "67+ Revealing Smartphone Statistics for 2021," *Techjury*, January 4, 2022, https://techjury.net/blog/smartphone-usage-statistics/#gref.

6. Trevor Wheelwright, "2022 Cell Phone Usage: How Obsessed Are We?," *Reviews.org*, January 24, 2022, www.reviews.org/mobile/cell-phone-addiction.

7. Ibid.

8. John Brandon, "New Survey Says We're Spending 7 Hours per Day Consuming Online Media," *Forbes*, November 17, 2020, www.forbes.com/sites /johnbbrandon/2020/11/17/new-survey-says-were-spending-7-hours-per-day -consuming-online-media/?sh=408eed776b46.

9. Statista Research Department, "Daily Time Spent on Social Networking by Internet Users Worldwide from 2021 to 2020," Statista, September 7, 2021, www.statista.com/statistics/433871/daily-social-media-usage-worldwide.

10. K. Kobayashi and M. Hsu, "Common Neural Code for Reward and Information Value," *PNAS* 116, no. 26 (2019): 13061–13066.

11. J. Litman, "Curiosity as a Feeling of Interest and Feeling of Deprivation: The I/D Model of Curiosity," in *Issues in the Psychology of Motivation*, ed. P. Zelick (New York: Nova Science Publishers, 2007).

12. T. Kashdan and M. Steger, "Curiosity and Pathways to Well-Being and Meaning in Life: Traits, States, and Everyday Behaviors," *Motivation and Emotion* 31, no. 3 (2007): 159–173; T. Kashdan, P. Rose, and F. Fincham, "Curiosity and Exploration: Facilitating Positive Subjective Experiences and Personal Growth Opportunities," *Journal of Personality Assessment* 82, no. 3 (2004): 291–305; T. Kashdan and J. Roberts, "Trait and State Curiosity in the Genesis of Intimacy: Differentiation from Related Constructs," *Journal of Social and Clinical Psychology* 23, no. 6 (2004): 792–816; G. E. Swan and D. Carmelli, "Curiosity and Mortality in Aging Adults: A 5-Year Follow-Up of the Western Collaborative Group Study," *Psychology and Aging* 11, no. 3 (1996): 449–453.

CHAPTER 1: UNCOVER YOUR ITCH TO KNOW

1. Mike Wall, "Rocket Lab Will Launch 30 Satellites and Attempt a Booster Recovery Today: Watch Live," *Space.com*, November 19, 2020, www.space.com /rocket-lab-launch-booster-recovery-return-to-sender-webcast.

2. "Rocket Lab USA Poised to Change the Space Industry," Rocket Lab, www.rocketlabusa.com/about-us/updates/rocket-lab-usa-poised-to-change -the-space-industry, accessed January 21, 2022; Meghan Bartels, "Rocket Lab Just Unveiled Plans for a Big New Rocket Called Neutron That Could Fly Astronauts," *Space.com*, March 1, 2021, www.space.com/rocket-lab-unveils -neutron-rocket-company-going-public.

3. Jackie Wattles, "NASA Says Moon Rocket Could Cost as Much as $1.6 Billion per Launch," *CNN Business*, December 9, 2019, https://edition.cnn.com/2019/12/09/tech/nasa-sls-price-cost-artemis-moon-rocket-scn/index.html; Jamie Smith, "Private Group in 'World First' Cheap Rocket Launch," *Financial Times*, January 21, 2018, www.ft.com/content/41572f8a-fe4d-11e7-9650-9c0ad2d7c5b5.

4. Wikipedia, s.v., "Rocket Lab Electron," updated March 21, 2022, https://en.wikipedia.org/wiki/Rocket_Lab_Electron.

5. Mike Wall, "Rocket Lab on Road to Reusability After Successful Booster Recovery," *Space.com*, November 24, 2020, www.space.com/rocket-lab-booster-recovery-success-for-reusability; Devin Coldewey, "Rocket Lab Makes Its First Booster Recovery After Successful Launch," *TechCrunch*, November 20, 2020, https://techcrunch.com/2020/11/19/rocket-lab-makes-its-first-booster-recovery-after-successful-launch.

6. "How to Bring a Rocket Back from Space," Rocket Lab, accessed January 21, 2022, www.rocketlabusa.com/updates/how-to-bring-a-rocket-back-from-space.

7. Peter Beck, interview with author, February 27, 2018.

8. Ibid.

9. Ashley Vance, "At 18, He Strapped a Rocket Engine to His Bike. Now He's Taking on Space X," *Bloomberg Businessweek*, June 29, 2017, www.bloomberg.com/news/features/2017-06-29/at-18-he-strapped-a-rocket-engine-to-his-bike-now-he-s-taking-on-spacex.

10. Bloomberg Quicktake: Originals, "Rocket Lab Is Giving SpaceX a Run for Its Money," video, YouTube, July 19, 2018, www.youtube.com/watch?v=DVdwtmFYyms&feature=emb_logo.

11. Jamie Smyth, "Private Group in 'World's First' Cheap Rocket Launch," *Financial Times*, January 21, 2018, www.ft.com/content/41572f8a-fe4d-11e7-9650-9c0ad2d7c5b5; Oliver Hitchens, "3D-Printed Rocket Engines: The Technology Driving the Private Sector Space Race," *Space.com*, September 28, 2021, www.space.com/3d-printed-rocket-engines-private-space-technology.

12. Ibid.

13. Devin Coldewey, "Rocket Lab Makes Its First Booster Recovery After Successful Launch," *TechCrunch*, November 20, 2020, https://techcrunch.com/2020/11/19/rocket-lab-makes-its-first-booster-recovery-after-successful-launch.

14. National Aeronautics and Space Administration, "Mach 2 and Beyond," NASA, updated October 13, 2020, www.nasa.gov/centers/armstrong/images/mach2/index.html.

15. Devin Coldewey, "'Complete Success': Rocket Lab's Booster Recovery Is a Big Step Toward Reusability," *TechCrunch*, November 24, 2020, https://techcrunch.com/2020/11/24/complete-success-rocket-labs-booster-recovery-is-a-big-step-towards-reusability.

16. Wall, "Rocket Lab on Road to Reusability."

17. Ibid.

18. Daniel Willingham, "Why Aren't We Curious About the Things We Want to Be Curious About?," *New York Times*, October 18, 2019, www.nytimes.com/2019/10/18/opinion/sunday/curiosity-brain.html.

19. Gillian Brockell, "During a Pandemic, Isaac Newton Had to Work from Home, Too. He Used the Time Wisely," *Washington Post*, March 12, 2020, www.washingtonpost.com/history/2020/03/12/during-pandemic-isaac-newton-had-work-home-too-he-used-time-wisely.

20. Thomas Levenson, "The Truth About Isaac Newton's Productive Plague," *New Yorker*, April 6, 2020, www.newyorker.com/culture/cultural-comment/the-truth-about-isaac-newtons-productive-plague.

21. Jólan van der Wiel, interview with author, February 15, 2018.

22. T. Wilson, D. Reinhard, E. Westgate, D. Gilbert, N. Ellerbeck, C. Hahn, C. Brown, and A. Shaked, "Just Think: The Challenges of the Disengaged Mind," *Science* 345, no. 6192 (2014): 75–77.

23. Auriea Harvey, interview with author, October 2, 2018.

24. Wilson et al., "Just Think."

25. Mitch Waldrop, "Inside Einstein's Love Affair with 'Lina'—His Cherished Violin," *National Geographic*, February 3, 2017, www.nationalgeographic.com/news/2017/02/einstein-genius-violin-music-physics-science.

26. Rob Dunn, "Painting with Penicillin: Alexander Fleming's Germ Art," *Smithsonian Magazine*, July 11, 2010, www.smithsonianmag.com/science-nature/painting-with-penicillin-alexander-flemings-germ-art-1761496.

27. Angelo Vermeulen, interview with author, June 18, 2018.

28. Jon Wiley, interview with author, June 11, 2018.

29. Ibid.

30. Sean Ness, interview with author, September 19, 2018.

31. Ibid.

32. Mary Katrantzou, interview with author, June 26, 2020.

33. Michael Jager, "Saving Curiosity," TEDxMiddlebury, November 2017, www.ted.com/talks/michael_jager_saving_curiosity.

34. Michael Jager, interview with author, September 25, 2020.

35. Ibid.

36. Jess Butcher, interview with author, September 5, 2018.

37. Marshall Culpepper, interview with author, April 2, 2018.

38. Roberta Lucca, interview with author, November 30, 2018.

39. Ibid.

40. Daisy Jacobs, interview with author, April 1, 2020.

41. Ibid.

42. Ibid.

43. E. O'Brien, "Enjoy It Again: Repeat Experiences Are Less Repetitive Than People Think," *Journal of Personality and Social Psychology* 116, no. 4 (2019): 519–540.

44. George Kourounis, interview with author, November 23, 2017.

45. George Kourounis, "Q&A: The First-Ever Expedition to Turkmenistan's 'Door to Hell,'" *National Geographic*, July 17, 2014, www.national geographic.com/adventure/article/140716-door-to-hell-darvaza-crater-george -kourounis-expedition.

46. Ibid.

47. Kourounis, interview with author.

48. Wikipedia, s.v. "Quantopian," updated March 27, 2022, https://en .wikipedia.org/wiki/Quantopian.

49. John Fawcett, interview with author, April 11, 2018.

50. Ibid.

51. P. Silvia, "What Is Interesting? Exploring the Appraisal Structure," *Emotion* 5, no. 1 (2005): 89–102.

52. Norman Foster, interview with author, April 26, 2018.

53. Ibid.

54. "Odisha Liveable Habitat Mission Won Bronze at World Habitat Awards," Norman Foster Foundation, December 10, 2019, www.normanfoster foundation.org/odisha-liveable-habitat-mission-won-bronze-at-world-habitat -awards; "Odisha Liveable Habitat Mission," World Habitat Awards, 2019, https://world-habitat.org/world-habitat-awards/winners-and-finalists/odisha -liveable-habitat-mission.

55. Raia Hadsell, interview with author, June 7, 2016.

56. Ibid.

57. Raphaël Domjan, interview with author, January 9, 2018.

58. Auriea Harvey, interview with author, October 2, 2018.

59. Kaggle, "2018 Data Science Bowl," accessed January 22, 2022, www .kaggle.com/c/data-science-bowl-2018/overview/about.

60. Cat Zakrzweski, "Hedge Fund Analysts Use Deep Learning to Diagnose Heart's Condition," *Wall Street Journal*, March 30, 2016, www.wsj.com /articles/BL-VCDB-18824.

61. Kaggle, "2018 Data Science Bowl."

62. Tencia Lee, interview with author, September 7, 2016.

63. Martin Frost, interview with author, January 4, 2019.

64. Ibid.

65. Vern Brownell, interview with author, June 13, 2018.

66. Silvia, "What Is Interesting?"

67. Ibid.

68. Tencia Lee, interview with author, September 7, 2016.

69. Angelo Vermeulen, interview with author, June 18, 2018.

CHAPTER 2: GO DOWN THE RABBIT HOLE: HABITS OF CURIOUS PEOPLE

1. Alice George, "Thank This World War II–Era Film Star for Your Wi-Fi," *Smithsonian Magazine*, April 4, 2019, www.smithsonianmag.com/smithsonian -institution/thank-world-war-ii-era-film-star-your-wi-fi-180971584.

2. Colleen Cheslak, "Hedy Lamar (1914–2000)," National Women's History Museum, 2018, www.womenshistory.org/education-resources/biographies/hedy -lamarr.

3. Joyce Bedi, "A Movie Star, Some Player Pianos, and Torpedoes," Lemelson Center for the Study of Invention and Innovation, Smithsonian National Museum of American History, November 12, 2015, https://invention.si.edu /movie-star-some-player-pianos-and-torpedoes.

4. George, "World War II–Era Film Star."

5. Gilbert King, "Team Hollywood's Secret Weapons System," *Smithsonian Magazine*, May 23, 2012, www.smithsonianmag.com/history/team-hollywoods -secret-weapons-system-103619955.

6. David Brancaccio and Paulina Velasco, "The Story of Hedy Lamarr, the Hollywood Beauty Whose Invention Helped Enable Wi-Fi, GPS and Bluetooth," *Marketplace*, November 21, 2017, www.marketplace.org/2017/11/21 /inventor-changed-our-world-and-also-happened-be-famous-hollywood-star.

7. Don Wilson, interview with author, June 15, 2017.

8. Ibid.

9. Anand Anandkumar, interview with author, March 27, 2019.

10. Ibid.

11. Ibid.

12. E. T. Higgins, A. W. Kruglanski, and A. Pierro, "Regulatory Mode: Locomotion and Assessment as Distinct Orientations," in *Advances in Experimental Social Psychology*, vol. 35, ed. M. P. Zanna (New York: Academic Press, 2003), 293–344.

13. Brett Lovelady, interview with author, September 10, 2020.

14. Ibid.

15. Wikipedia, s.v. "Gavin Turk," updated March 28, 2022, https://en .wikipedia.org/wiki/Gavin_Turk.

16. Ibid.

17. "Biography," GavinTurk.com, accessed March 31, 2022, http://gavinturk .com/biography.

18. Gavin Turk, interview with author, May 1, 2020.

19. Ibid.

20. "About," FelicityAston.co.uk, accessed March 31, 2020, www.felicity aston.co.uk/about.

21. Felicity Aston, interview with author, April 12, 2019.

22. H. Klein, R. Lount Jr., H. M. Park, and B. J. Linford, "When Goals Are Known: The Effects of Audience Relative Status on Goal Commitment and Performance," *Journal of Applied Psychology* 105, no. 4 (2020): 372–389.

23. Andy Bull, "Ben Saunders: Explorer, Adventurer, Speck of Red Heat," *Guardian*, March 13, 2008, www.theguardian.com/sport/2008/mar/13/andybull.

24. Ben Saunders, interview with author, April 12, 2017.

25. Gever Tulley, interview with author, February 6, 2019.

26. Ibid.

27. Cliff Jones, "Why Low-Tech and Outdoor Play Is Trending in Education," *Financial Times*, June 22, 2018, www.ft.com/content/7ad7d6ec-5393-11e8 -84f4-43d65af59d43.

28. Maximilian Büsser, interview with author, September 17, 2020.

29. Ibid.

30. Ibid.

31. Marshall Culpepper, interview with author, April 2, 2018.

CHAPTER 3: CONQUER YOUR FEARS WITH CURIOSITY

1. Britannica, s.v. "Antarctica, Continent," updated March 12, 2022, www.britannica.com/place/Antarctica.

2. "Kaspersky ONE Trans-Antarctic Expedition," FelicityAston.co.uk accessed March 31, 2022, www.felicityaston.co.uk/kaspersky-one.

3. Felicity Aston, interview with author, April 12, 2019.

4. Ibid.

5. Ibid.

6. "About British Antarctic Survey," British Antarctic Survey, Natural Environment Research Council, accessed March 31, 2022, www.bas.ac.uk/about/about-bas.

7. Julia Savacool, "Felicity Aston Conquers Fears, Antarctica," *ESPN*, March 20, 2012, www.espn.com/espnw/journeys-victories/story/_/id/7710393/british-adventurer-felicity-aston-conquers-fears-antarctica.

8. Aston, interview with author.

9. Ibid.

10. Ibid.

11. Savacool, "Felicity Aston Conquers Fears."

12. Ibid.

13. Aston, interview with author.

14. Robert Booth, "Briton Felicity Aston Becomes First to Manually Ski Solo Across Antarctica," *Guardian*, January 23, 2012, www.theguardian.com/world/2012/jan/23/felicity-aston-ski-solo-antarctica.

15. Aston, interview with author.

16. "About," FelicityAston.co.uk, accessed March 31, 2022, www.felicityaston.co.uk/about.

17. Louis Cozolino, "Nine Things Educators Need to Know About the Brain," *Greater Good Magazine*, March 19, 2013, https://greatergood.berkeley.edu/article/item/nine_things_educators_need_to_know_about_the_brain.

18. George Kourounis, interview with author, November 23, 2017.

19. Z. Bauman, *Liquid Fear* (Cambridge, MA: Polity Press, 2006), 2.

20. Wesley Grover, "How to Overcome Isolation and Self-Doubt, According to Polar Explorer Felicity Aston," *Men's Journal*, accessed January 20, 2022, www.mensjournal.com/adventure/how-to-overcome-self-doubt-and-loneliness-in-isolation.

21. P. R. Clance and S. Imes, "The Imposter Phenomenon in High Achieving Women: Dynamics and Therapeutic Intervention," *Psychotherapy Theory, Research and Practice* 15, no. 3 (1978): 241–247; Ellen Hendriksen, "What Is Impostor Syndrome?," *Scientific American*, May 27, 2015, www.scientificamerican.com/article/what-is-impostor-syndrome.

22. Rose Leadem, "12 Leaders, Entrepreneurs and Celebrities Who Have Struggled with Imposter Syndrome," *Entrepreneur*, November 8, 2017, www.entrepreneur.com/slideshow/304273#2.

23. Kourounis, interview with author.

24. Daisy Jacobs, interview with author, April 1, 2020.

25. Ibid.

26. Emily Ford, "Daisy Jacobs Missed Out on an Oscar for Her Short Film *The Bigger Picture*," *Southern Daily Echo*, February 23, 2015, www.dailyecho.co.uk/news/11810714.daisy-jacobs-missed-out-on-an-oscar-for-her-short-film-the-bigger-picture.

27. Jacobs, interview with author.

28. Ibid.

29. TED Blog Video, "Two Monkeys Were Paid Unequally: Excerpt from Frans de Waal's TED Talk," video, YouTube, April 4, 2013, www.youtube.com/watch?v=meiU6TxysCg.

30. For the curiosity scale, see T. B. Kashdan, M. G. Gallagher, P. J. Silvia, B. Winterstein, W. E. Breen, D. Terhar, and M. F. Steger, "The Curiosity and Exploration Inventory, II: Development, Factor Structure, and Psychometrics," *Journal of Research in Personality* 43, no. 6 (2009): 987–998. For the Kawamoto et al. study, see T. Kawamoto, M. Ura, and K. Hiraki, "Curious People Are Less Affected by Social Rejection," *Personality and Individual Differences* 105 (2017): 264–267.

31. Maximilian Büsser, interview with author, September 17, 2020.

32. G. T. Fairhurst and R. A. Starr, *The Art of Framing: Managing the Language of Leadership* (San Francisco: Jossey-Bass, 1996).

33. John Fawcett, interview with author, April 11, 2018.

34. "Meet Michael," Michael Robotham.com, accessed January 20, 2022, www.michaelrobotham.com/Index.asp?pagename=Meet+Michael&site=1 &siteid=9494.

35. Ayo Onatade, "Michael Robotham Interview," *Shots, Crime & Thriller Ezine*, accessed January 20, 2022, www.shotsmag.co.uk/interview_view.aspx ?interview_id=158.

36. "Frequently Asked Questions," Michael Robotham.com, accessed January 20, 2022, www.michaelrobotham.com/index.asp?pagename=FAQ&site =1&siteid=9494.

37. Wikipedia, s.v. "Michael Robotham," updated February 4, 2022, https:// en.wikipedia.org/wiki/Michael_Robotham.

38. Michael Robotham, interview with author, September 16, 2020.

39. Ibid.

40. This discussion of Lucca and the various companies she founded come from Roberta Lucca, interview with author, November 30, 2018.

41. Wikipedia, s.v. "Multipotentiality," updated March 17, 2022, https:// en.wikipedia.org/wiki/Multipotentiality; Emilie Wapnick, "Why Some of Us Don't Have One True Calling," video, TEDxBend, April 2015, www.ted.com/talks /emilie_wapnick_why_some_of_us_don_t_have_one_true_calling/up-next ?language=en.

42. J. Morrens, C. Aydin, A. Janse van Rensburg, J. Esquivelzeta Rabell, and S. Haesler, "Cue-Evoked Dopamine Promotes Conditioned Responding During Learning," *Neuron* 106, no. 1 (2020): 142–153.

43. Roberta Lucca, interview with author, November 30, 2018.

44. Daemon Fairless, Mark Gollom, and Chris Oke, "Hunting Warhead," *CBC News*, December 18, 2019, https://newsinteractives.cbc.ca/longform /hunting-warhead-child-porn-investigation.

45. Håkon Høydal, interview with author, June 11, 2016.

46. Fiona Sturges, "Hunting Warhead: A New Podcast Series That Shines a Light on the 'Dark Web,'" *Financial Times*, November 10, 2019, www.ft.com /content/a113b246-0214-11ea-a530-16c6c29e70ca.

47. Høydal, interview with author.

48. Ibid.

49. Håkon Høydal and Christina Quist, "This Map Shows 95,000 Down-loaders of Child Abuse Pictures Worldwide," *VG*, December 17, 2015, www .vg.no/nyheter/innenriks/i/PM9V0/this-map-shows-95000-downloaders-of -child-abuse-pictures-worldwide.

50. Fairless, Gollom, and Oke, "Hunting Warhead."

51. Høydal, interview with author.

52. Hans Guyt, "This Statement to the Human Rights Council in Geneva by Norwegian Journalist Håkon Høydal Makes for Fascinating Reading," LinkedIn, March 9, 2016, www.linkedin.com/pulse/statement-human-rights-council-geneva-investigative-norwegian-guyt.

53. Wikipedia, s.v. "Nicole Cooke," updated March 10, 2022, https://en.wikipedia.org/wiki/Nicole_Cooke.

54. Nicole Cooke, interview with author, March 11, 2014.

55. Ibid.

56. Ibid.

57. Wikipedia, s.v. "Nicole Cooke."

58. Ibid.

59. Ibid.

60. John Underkoffler, "Pointing to the Future of UI," TED2010, February 2010, www.ted.com/talks/john_underkoffler_pointing_to_the_future_of_ui/transcript; Darren Clarke, "MIT Grad Directs Spielberg in the Science of Moviemaking," MIT News, July 17, 2002, https://news.mit.edu/2002/underkoffler-0717.

61. Tom Ward, "The Mind Behind Minority Report Is Giving PowerPoint a Sci-Fi Overhaul," Wired, March 12, 2019, www.wired.co.uk/article/oblong-minority-report-john-underkoffler.

62. Ibid.

63. John Underkoffler, interview with author, March 7, 2019.

CHAPTER 4: BECOME AN EXPERT—FAST

1. Marshall Culpepper, interview with author, April 2, 2018.

2. Marshall Culpepper, "Kubos Raises $375K for Open Source Satellite Platform," Medium, March 11, 2016, https://medium.com/kubos-tech/kubos-raises-375k-seed-round-for-open-source-satellite-platform-58b3b5257a06.

3. Culpepper, interview with author.

4. Vern Brownell, interview with author, June 13, 2018.

5. Ibid.

6. "About Us," Office Group, accessed February 4, 2022, www.theofficegroup.com/uk/about-us.

7. Olly Olsen, interview with author, May 15, 2017.

8. Hazel Forsyth, interview with author, May 12, 2017.

9. Wikipedia, s.v. "ArXiv," updated February 16, 2022, https://en.wikipedia.org/wiki/ArXiv.

10. "About the Concealed Histories Display," Victoria and Albert Museum, accessed February 8, 2022, www.vam.ac.uk/articles/about-the-concealed-histories-display#slideshow=6872&slide=0.

11. Jacques Schuhmacher, interview with author, March 13, 2020.

12. Vern Brownell, interview with author, June 13, 2018.

13. Lionel Barber, interview with author, January 17, 2019.

14. Ibid.

15. Jólan van der Wiel, interview with author, February 15, 2018.

16. Gavin Turk, interview with author, May 1, 2020.

17. Ibid.

18. Underkoffler, interview with author.

19. Martin Frost, interview with author, January 4, 2019.

20. Roman Krznaric, "Six Habits of Highly Empathic People," *Greater Good Magazine*, November 27, 2012, https://greatergood.berkeley.edu/article/item/six_habits_of_highly_empathic_people1.

21. E. Boothby, G. Cooney, G. Sandstrom, and M. Clark, "The Liking Gap in Conversations: Do People Like Us More Than We Think?," *Psychological Science* 29, no. 11 (2018): 1742–1756.

22. G. Sandstrom and E. Dunn, "Social Interactions and Well-Being: The Surprising Power of Weak Ties," *Personality and Social Psychology Bulletin* 40, no. 7 (2014): 910–922.

23. Ben Saunders, interview with author, April 12, 2017.

24. Ibid.

25. T. Kashdan, P. McKnight, F. Fincham, and P. Rose, "When Curiosity Breeds Intimacy: Taking Advantage of Intimacy Opportunities and Transforming Boring Conversations," *Journal of Personality* 79, no. 6 (2011): 1369–1402.

26. Nigel Toon, interview with author, January 9, 2018.

27. T. Kashdan and J. Roberts, "Trait and State Curiosity in the Genesis of Intimacy: Differentiation from Related Constructs," *Journal of Social and Clinical Psychology* 23, no. 6 (2005): 792–816.

28. Zowie Broach, interview with author, January 26, 2019.

29. Sam Bompas, interview with author, June 12, 2017.

30. Jon Wiley, interview with author, June 11, 2018.

31. Ibid.

32. The Biodesign Challenge (www.biodesignchallenge.org) is a global education program and international student competition that pairs high school and university students with artists, scientists, and designers to explore the future of biotechnology.

33. Louis Alderson-Bythell, interview with author, March 7, 2019.

34. "What's Behind the Decline in Bees and Other Pollinators?" European Parliament, updated June 9, 2021, www.europarl.europa.eu/news/en/headlines/society/20191129STO67758/what-s-behind-the-decline-in-bees-and-other-pollinators-infographic.

35. Ibid.

36. SVG Ventures, "Why We Invested: Olombria," *Thrive*, May 8, 2019.

37. Alderson-Bythell, interview with author.

38. Ibid.

39. Forsyth, interview with author.

40. Ibid.; Hazel Forsyth, *The Cheapside Hoard: London's Lost Jewels* (London: Philip Wilson Publishers, 2013).

41. Forsyth, interview with author.

42. Helen Forsyth, *Butcher, Baker, Candlestick Maker: Surviving the Great Fire of London* (London and New York: I.B. Tauris & Co, 2016).

43. Forsyth, interview with author.

44. Jacques Schuhmacher, interview with author, March 13, 2020.

45. Joseph Henrich, *The Secret of Our Success: How Culture Is Driving Human Evolution, Domesticating Our Species, and Making Us Smarter* (Princeton, NJ: Princeton University Press, 2015).

46. George Kourounis, interview with author, November 23, 2017.

47. Lionel Barber, interview with author, January 17, 2019.

48. Nigel Toon, interview with author, January 9, 2018.

49. Ben Saunders, interview with author, April 12, 2017.

50. Michael Robotham, interview with author, September 16, 2020.

51. Ibid.

52. Vern Brownell, interview with author, June 13, 2018.

CHAPTER 5: ASK, "WHO'S WITH ME?"

1. Thieme Hennis, interview with author, June 22, 2018.

2. "Border Sessions," Facebook, accessed February 2, 2022, www.facebook.com/CB.BorderSessions.

3. Hennis, interview with author.

4. "How It Began," European Space Agency, accessed February 7, 2022, www.esa.int/Enabling_Support/Space_Engineering_Technology/How_it_began.

5. Hennis, interview with author.

6. "Grow Plants in Space," AstroPlant, accessed February 2, 2022, https://astroplant.io.

7. Hennis, interview with author.

8. "Grow Plants in Space."

9. "Introduction to AstroPlant," AstroPlant, accessed February 2, 2022, https://docs.astroplant.io/getting-started/introduction-to-astroplant.

10. Hennis, interview with author.

11. Ibid.

12. Håkon Høydal, interview with author, June 11, 2018.

13. Yonatan Raz-Fridman, interview with author, June 14, 2016.

14. Roberta Lucca, interview with author, November 30, 2018.

15. Ben Saunders, interview with author, April 12, 2017.

16. Ibid.

17. Todd Kashdan, "Companies Value Curiosity but Stifle It Anyway," *Harvard Business Review*, October 21, 2015, https://hbr.org/2015/10/companies-value-curiosity-but-stifle-it-anyway.

18. Ibid.

19. I. L. Janis, *Victims of Groupthink: A Psychological Study of Foreign-Policy Decisions and Fiascoes* (New York: Houghton Mifflin,1972).

20. "About Us," MaryKatrantzou.com, accessed February 2, 2022, www.marykatrantzou.com/about.

21. Ibid.

22. Mary Katrantzou, interview with author, June 26, 2020.

23. Ibid.

24. Alexus Graham, "SCAD FASH's Latest Exhibition Showcases Mary Katrantzou's Lush Fashions," *Atlantan*, August 9, 2019, https://atlantanmagazine.com/scad-fash-exhibit-mary-katrantzou.

25. Katrantzou, interview with author.

26. Sam Bompas, interview with author, June 12, 2017.

27. Jon Wiley, interview with author, June 11, 2018.

28. Ibid.

29. Ceylan Shevket, interview with author, June 7, 2017.

30. Pete Bottomley, interview with author, February 13, 2019.

31. Ibid.

32. Bompas, interview with author.

33. A. Aron, C. Norman, E. N. Aron, C. McKenna, and R. E. Heyman, "Couples' Shared Participation in Novel and Arousing Activities and Experienced Relationship Quality," *Journal of Personality and Social Psychology* 78, no. 2 (2000): 273–284.

34. Giampaolo Dallara, interview with author, March 19, 2019.

35. Ibid.; Wikipedia, s.v. "Gian Paolo Dallara," updated March 9, 2022, https://en.wikipedia.org/wiki/Gian_Paolo_Dallara.

36. Dallara, interview with author.

37. Ibid.

38. "Edmund Hillary and Tenzing Norgay Reach Everest Summit," *History*, accessed February 8, 2022, www.history.com/this-day-in-history/hillary-and-tenzing-reach-everest-summit.

39. Mick Conefrey, *Everest 1953: The Epic Story of the First Ascent* (London: Oneworld Publications, 2013).

40. Ibid.

CHAPTER 6: GET READY

1. Ben Saunders, "Polar and Arctic Environments," *Royal Geographic Society Explore 2016*, November 19, 2016.

2. For the Shackleton expedition, see Patricia Brennan, "Shackleton's Successful Failure," *Washington Post*, March 24, 2002, www.washingtonpost.com/archive/lifestyle/tv/2002/03/24/shackletons-successful-failure/4c72b4b9-da9f-4bc4-93cc-ed4626d79509. For the Scott expedition, see "What Went Wrong for Captain Scott and His Team to Die on the Way Back from the South Pole?," Cool Antarctica, accessed February 8, 2022, www.coolantarctica.com/Antarctica%20fact%20file/History/Robert-Falcon-Scott-death-reasons.php.

3. Saunders, "Polar and Arctic Environments."

4. Ibid.

5. Ben Saunders, interview with author, April 12, 2017.

6. Ibid.

7. "Adventure Stats Polar Rules and Definitions," Explorersweb, accessed February 3, 2022, https://explorersweb.com/stats/news.php?id=20374.

8. Alicia Clegg, "Polar Explorer Ben Saunders Embraces His Failures," *Financial Times*, April 27, 2018, www.ft.com/content/8dd4c332-42f3-11e8-97ce-ea0c2bf34a0b.

9. Saunders, interview with author.

10. Ibid.

11. Saunders, "Polar and Arctic Environments."

12. Saunders, interview with author.

13. R. Buehler, D. Griffin, and M. Ross, "Exploring the 'Planning Fallacy': Why People Underestimate Their Task Completion Times," *Journal of Personality and Social Psychology* 67, no. 3 (1994): 366–381.

14. Daniel Shea, "Raphaël Domjan," OnboardOnline, February 12, 2013, www.onboardonline.com/superyacht-news/interviews/raphael-domjan.

15. Deborah Netburn, "Solar-Powered Catamaran Goes Around the World in 584 Days," *Los Angeles Times*, May 4, 2012, www.latimes.com/business/la-xpm-2012-may-04-la-fi-tn-solar-powered-catamaran-goes-around-the-world-in-584-days-20120504-story.html.

16. Henry Fountain, "Solar Boat Harnessed for Research," *New York Times*, June 24, 2013, www.nytimes.com/2013/06/25/science/solar-boat-harnessed-for-research.html.

17. Felicity Aston, interview with author, April 12, 2019.

18. Gary Klein, "Performing a Project Premortem," *Harvard Business Review* 85, no. 9 (2007): 18–19.

19. Ibid.

20. Aston, interview with author.

21. Thieme Hennis, interview with author, June 22, 2018.

22. Peter Beck, interview with author, February 27, 2018.

23. Ceylan Shevket, interview with author, June 7, 2017.

24. Claudia Pasquero, interview with author, June 22, 2018.

25. Ibid.

26. Raia Hadsell, interview with author, June 7, 2016.

27. Anna Marks, "This Pollution-Busting Window Cleans the Air with Photosynthesis," *Wired*, April 30, 2019, www.wired.co.uk/article/cities-air-pollution-clean-photosynthesis.

28. Nicole Cooke, interview with author, March 11, 2014.

29. Chen Reiss, interview with author, December 27, 2017.

30. Saunders, interview with author.

31. Aston, interview with author.

32. Reiss, interview with author.

CHAPTER 7: LEAP INTO THE UNKNOWN

1. Sean O'Grady, "Earl of March: A Glorious Example of the Landed Classes," *Independent* (London), July 30, 2009, www.independent.co.uk/news /people/profiles/earl-of-march-a-glorious-example-of-the-landed-classes-1764664 .html.

2. Richard.Bellis, "Here's Some of the Famous Alumni of Eton College," *Northern Echo* (UK), July 21, 2021, www.thenorthernecho.co.uk/news/19455798 .famous-alumni-eton-college.

3. Katie Law, "Charles March on Being Both a Duke and a Celebrated Photographer," *Evening Standard* (London), October 12, 2017, www.standard.co .uk/culture/charles-march-on-being-both-a-duke-and-a-celebrated-photographer -a3656841.html.

4. Ibid.; Kat Herriman, "Lord Charles March Goes into the Woods, *W Magazine*, January 22, 2015, www.wmagazine.com/story/lord-charles-march -photography.

5. "Our History," Goodwood, accessed February 7, 2022, www.goodwood .com/estate/our-history.

6. Charles Gordon-Lennox, interview with author, April 27, 2018.

7. Ibid.

8. "Freddie March—Driving Ambition," Goodwood, accessed February 7, 2022, www.goodwood.com/estate/our-history.

9. Ibid.

10. Ibid. "Remembering 'Mr Goodwood': Sir Stirling Moss," Goodwood, accessed February 8, 2022, www.goodwood.com/grr/race/historic/2020/4 /remembering-mr-goodwood-sir-stirling-moss.

11. Charles Gordon-Lennox, interview with author, April 27, 2018.

12. Ibid.

13. Raphaël Domjan, interview with author, January 9, 2018.

14. For statistics on incomplete dissertations, see Lea Winerman, "Ten Years to a Doctorate? Not Anymore," *American Psychological Association*, March 2008, www.apa.org/gradpsych/2008/03/cover-doctorate. For the range of reasons, see Lise Dyckman, "Fear of Failure and Fear of Finishing: A Case Study on the Emo-

tional Aspects of Dissertation Proposal Research, with Thoughts on Library Instruction and Graduate Student Retention," Association of College and Research Libraries Twelfth National Conference, Minneapolis, April 7–10, 2005, www .ala.org/acrl/sites/ala.org.acrl/files/content/conferences/pdf/dyckman05.pdf.

15. George Kourounis, interview with author, November 23, 2017.

16. Nigel Toon, interview with author, January 9, 2018.

17. Raviv Drucker, interview with author, September 3, 2018.

18. Martin Frost, interview with author, January 4, 2019.

19. Zowie Broach, interview with author, January 26, 2019.

20. Joao Medeiros, "The Science Behind Chris Froome and Team Sky's Tour de France Preparations," *Wired*, June 30, 2016, www.wired.co.uk/article /tour-de-france-science-behind-team-sky.

21. Ben Saunders, interview with author, April 12, 2017.

22. Daisy Jacobs, interview with author, April 1, 2020.

23. Don Wilson, interview with author, June 15, 2017.

24. Ibid.

25. Zowie Broach, interview with author, January 26, 2019.

26. Lionel Barber, interview with author, January 17, 2019.

27. Felicity Aston, interview with author, April 12, 2019.

28. Håkon Høydal, interview with author, June 11, 2018.

29. Ibid.

30. Ibid.

31. Vern Brownell, interview with author, June 13, 2018.

32. Charles Gordon-Lennox, interview with author, April 27, 2018.

33. Brownell, interview with author.

34. Jon Wiley, interview with author, June 11, 2018.

35. Kourounis, interview with author.

36. Zar Amrolia, interview with author, May 4, 2018.

37. Ibid.

38. Barber, interview with author.

CHAPTER 8: DEVELOP RESILIENCE IN THE FACE OF ADVERSITY

1. Hazel Forsyth, interview with author, May 12, 2017.

2. "The Great Fire of London," Monument, accessed January 26, 2022, www.themonument.org.uk/great-fire-london-faqs.

3. Forsyth, interview with author.

4. Ibid.

5. Ibid.

6. Ibid.

7. Helen Forsyth, *Butcher, Baker, Candlestick Maker: Surviving the Great Fire of London* (London and New York: I.B. Tauris & Co, 2016).

8. Bari Walsh, "The Science of Resilience: Why Some Children Can Thrive Despite Adversity," *Usable Knowledge* (Harvard Graduate School of Education), March 23, 2015, www.gse.harvard.edu/news/uk/15/03/science-resilience.

9. Kazuhide Sekiyama, "Proteins for Peace: A Chance Discovery in Advanced Biosciences Research," *Keio Times* (Keio University), October 29, 2021, www.keio.ac.jp/en/keio-times/features/2021/9.

10. Kazuhide Sekiyama, interview with author, April 1, 2019.

11. Kana Inagaki, "Spider Man: Kazuhide Sekiyama, Spiber," *Financial Times*, March 1, 2016, www.ft.com/content/e8e55656-c8cf-11e5-be0b-b7ece4e953a0.

12. "Brewed Protein," Spiber Inc., accessed January 26, 2022, https://spiber.inc/en/brewedprotein.

13. "Spiber Inc. Raises JPY 34.4 Billion in Funding to Strengthen Production and Sales Network," *Business Wire*, September 8, 2021, www.businesswire.com/news/home/20210908005992/en/Spiber-Inc.-Raises-JPY-34.4-Billion-in-Funding-to-Strengthen-Production-and-Sales-Network.

14. "Contributing to Sustainable Well-Being," Spiber Inc., accessed January 26, 2022, https://spiber.inc/en/about.

15. Kazuhide Sekiyama, interview with author, April 1, 2019.

16. Raviv Drucker, interview with author, September 3, 2018.

17. Chen Reiss, interview with author, December 27, 2017.

18. Ibid.

19. Håkon Høydal, interview with author, June 11, 2018.

20. M. Wittman, N. Kolling, N. Faber, J. Scholl, N. Nelissen, and M. Rushworth, "Self-Other Mergence in the Frontal Cortex During Cooperation and Competition," *Neuron* 91 (2016): 482–493.

21. "Adrian Newey OBE," Red Bull Racing, accessed January 26, 2022, www.redbullracing.com/int-en/drivers/adrian-newey-obe.

22. Ibid.

23. Wikipedia, s.v. "Adrian Newey," accessed March 26, 2022, https://en.wikipedia.org/wiki/Adrian_Newey.

24. "Adrian Newey," Formula One Wiki, accessed January 26, 2022, https://f1history.fandom.com/wiki/Adrian_Newey.

25. "Adrian Newey OBE."

26. "Adrian Newey," Formula One Wiki, accessed January 26, 2022, https://f1history.fandom.com/wiki/Adrian_Newey.

27. "Adrian Newey OBE."

28. Ibid.

29. Wikipedia, s.v. "Red Bull Racing," updated April 2, 2022, https://en.wikipedia.org/wiki/Red_Bull_Racing.

30. Oracle Red Bull Racing (@redbullracing) tweeted: "The win today also marks Adrian Newey's 150th win in Formula One! #BelgianGP," Twitter, August 24, 2014, https://twitter.com/redbullracing/status/503565864109883394?lang=en-GB.

31. Adrian Newey, interview with author, September 4, 2018.

32. Gershon Tenenbaum, interview with author, October 2, 2017.

33. M. Polk, E. Smith, L. Zhang, and S. Neupert, "Thinking Ahead and Staying in the Present: Implications for Reactivity to Daily Stressors," *Personality and Individual Differences* 161 (July 15, 2020), www.sciencedirect.com/science/article/pii/S0191886920301604.

34. Kate Morgan, "Why Making Plans Helps Manage Pandemic Stress," *BBC*, July 21, 2020, www.bbc.com/worklife/article/20200720-how-planning-helps-us-cope-with-uncertainty.

35. Polk et al., "Thinking Ahead."

36. P. M. Ullrich and S. K. Lutgendorf, "Journaling About Stressful Events: Effects of Cognitive Processing and Emotional Expression," *Annals of Behavioural Medicine* 24 (2002): 244–250.

37. K. K. Fritson, "Impact of Journaling on Students' Self-Efficacy and Locus of Control," *InSight: A Journal of Scholarly Teaching* 3 (2008): 75–83.

38. J. M. Smyth, J. A. Johnson, B. J. Auer, E. Lehman, G. Talamo, and C. N. Sciamanna, "Online Positive Affect Journaling in the Improvement of Mental Distress and Well-Being in General Medical Patients with Elevated Anxiety Symptoms: A Preliminary Randomized Controlled Trial," *JMIR Mental Health* 5, no. 4 (2018): e11290.

39. Gershon Tenenbaum, interview with author, October 2, 2017.

40. Peter Beck, interview with author, February 27, 2018.

41. Robert Ibbotson, interview with author, May 25, 2017.

42. Ibid.

CHAPTER 9: TURN THE ENDING INTO YOUR NEW BEGINNING

1. Wikipedia, s.v. "Mae Jemison," updated March 28, 2022, https://en.wikipedia.org/wiki/Mae_Jemison.

2. Jesse Katz, "Shooting Star," *Stanford Daily*, July–August 1996, https://web.stanford.edu/dept/news/stanfordtoday/ed/9607/pdf/ST9607mjemison.pdf.

3. Ibid.

4. "Dr. Mae C. Jemison," *Changing the Face of Medicine*, US National Library of Medicine, updated June 3, 2015, https://cfmedicine.nlm.nih.gov/physicians/biography_168.html.

5. "Mae C. Jemison Biography," Biography.com, updated July 15, 2021, www.biography.com/astronaut/mae-c-jemison.

6. Michael Jager, interview with author, September 25, 2020.

7. Mary Katrantzou, interview with author, June 26, 2020.

8. Gavin Turk, interview with author, May 1, 2020.

9. Edward Bonham Carter, interview with author, May 12, 2017.

10. Ibid.

11. Ibid.

12. Chen Reiss, interview with author, December 27, 2017.

13. Adrian Newey, interview with author, September 4, 2018.

14. Felicity Aston, interview with author, April 12, 2019; George Kourounis, interview with author, November 23, 2017; Ben Saunders, interview with author, April 12, 2017.

15. Don Wilson, interview with author, June 15, 2017.

16. Jean Folger, "Metaverse Definition," *Investopedia*, October 28, 2021, www.investopedia.com/metaverse-definition-5206578.

17. Kazuhide Sekiyama, interview with author, April 1, 2019.

18. Newey, interview with author.

19. Jager, interview with author.

20. Sekiyama, interview with author.

21. Rob Nail, interview with author, February 18, 2019.

22. Tom Gorman and Sanjena Sathian, "Robots and Utopia: Silicon Valley's Quirkiest CEO," OZY, August 12, 2015, www.ozy.com/news-and-politics/robots-and-utopia-silicon-valleys-quirkiest-ceo/40048.

23. Nail, interview with author.

24. Ibid.

25. Ibid.

26. Roberta Lucca, interview with author, November 30, 2018.

27. Auriea Harvey, interview with author, October 20, 2018.

28. Jess Butcher, interview with author, September 5, 2018.

29. Tencia Lee, interview with author, September 7, 2016.

30. William Harlan, interview with author, June 18, 2018.

31. Nicole Cooke, interview with author, March 11, 2014.

32. Rebecca Gibb, "Harlan Estate: A New Wine Dynasty," Deutsche Bank, June 5, 2019, https://deutschewealth.com/en/conversations/entrepreneurship/harlan-estate-the-next-wine-dynasty.html.

33. "Legacy," Pacific Union Partners, accessed February 8, 2022, https://pacunionpartners.com/our-company/legacy.

34. Adam Lechmere, "Bill Harlan: The Wild One," Club Oenologique, November 1, 2020, https://cluboenologique.com/story/bill-harlan-the-wild-one.

35. Adam Lechmere, "In Conversation with Bill Harlan," Wine Conversation, accessed February 8, 2022, www.wine-conversation.com/conversations/great-wine-lives-bill-harlan.

36. Judith Nasatir, *Observations from the Hillside* (St. Helena, CA: Harlan Estate, 2010).

37. "In Conversation with Bill Harlan," Wine Conversation, accessed February 8, 2022, www.wine-conversation.com/conversations/great-wine-lives-bill-harlan.

38. Nasatir, *Observations from the Hillside.*

39. The term *first growth* applies to wines in the Médoc and Graves region in France and means "first in class." There are five Bordeaux châteaus that are known as first growth: Haut-Brion, Lafite Rothschild, Mouton Rothschild, Latour, and Margaux.

40. Anthony Maxwell, "Liv-ex Interview with Bill Harlan, Part One: Napa Valley and the California First Growth," Liv-ex, August 23, 2018, www.liv-ex.com/2018/08/liv-ex-interview-bill-harlan-part-one-napa-valley-californian-first-growth.

41. Anthony Maxwell, "Liv-ex Interview with Bill Harlan, Part Two: Robert Parker and the Secondary Market," Liv-ex, August 23, 2018, www.liv-ex.com/2018/08/liv-ex-interview-bill-harlan-part-two-robert-parker-secondary-market.

42. Julia Flynn, "A Successful Vintner Pours His Passion into Dynastic Dream," *Wall Street Journal*, July 1, 2016, www.wsj.com/articles/SB1151721 40824696135#.

43. Nasatir, *Observations from the Hillside;* W. Blake Gray, "Harlan Estate's 200-Year Plan," Wine-Searcher, August 1, 2013, www.wine-searcher.com/m /2013/08/harlan-estates-200-year-plan.

44. Nasatir, *Observations from the Hillside.*

45. Ibid.

AFTERWORD

1. Hazel Forsyth, interview with author, May 12, 2017.

2. Michael Robotham, interview with author, September 16, 2020.

3. Leda Braga, interview with author, March 27, 2019.

4. Zar Amrolia, interview with author, May 4, 2018.

5. Adrian Newey, interview with author, September 4, 2018.

6. John Underkoffler, interview with author, March 7, 2019.

7. Edward Bonham Carter, interview with author, May 12, 2017.

8. Jess Butcher, interview with author, September 5, 2018.

9. Gever Tulley, interview with author, February 6, 2019.

10. Ben Saunders, interview with author, April 12, 2017.

11. Don Wilson, interview with author, June 15, 2017.

12. Raphaël Domjan, interview with author, January 9, 2018; Georgianna Hiliadaki, interview with author, December 14, 2017.

13. Caleb Kramer, interview with author, June 7, 2017.

14. Max Mersch, interview with author, March 28, 2018.

15. Georgianna Hiliadaki, interview with author, December 14, 2017.

16. Blaise Pascal, *Pensées and Other Writings* (Oxford: Oxford University Press, 1995; reissued 2008), 28.

17. Ma Yansong, interview with author, March 7, 2018.